FROM
POOP
TO
GOLD

THE MARKETING MAGIC
OF HARMON BROTHERS

CHRIS JONES

FIRST EDITION

Direct Inquiries to:
Harmon Brothers, LLC
410 S University Ave
Provo, UT 84601

Harmonbrothers.com

ISBN 978-0-692-04282-3

Library of Congress Control Number: 2018961892

Cover Design by Daniel Harmon
Interior design by Daniel Ruesch Design, Inc.
Caricatures by Alex Buie
Printed By PubLitho

Table of Contents

Foreward

by Bobby Edwards

I am the CEO of Squatty Potty, a company that went from small to large from one Harmon Brothers video.

Before Harmon Brothers, I knew Squatty Potty stools were funny. Poop things are funny. But my website was not funny. It was a photograph of a skeleton on the toilet using a Squatty Potty with the tagline, "Your Toilet Could Be Killing You." Dreaming of a Harmon Brothers video kept me up at night.

After appearing on *Shark Tank*, we finally had the money to fund an ad. We called up Jeffrey. "We want to do it. Get out the contract." "Good," he said, "Unicorns are starting to go crazy on the internet right now. We're going to do unicorn poop."

Once we started making the commercial, it was scary. We had gained some credibility in the alternative health world as a device that helped people medically. And we'd just connected to sell retail in Bed Bath & Beyond and Target. Now, we were handing over our reputation to a *unicorn*. Everything was on the line.

The video launched. And I was addicted to the screen, watching our order numbers. Our normal sales at that time were fifty a day. Post video, sales were nothing on the first day. The second day was our normal fifty orders. The third day, 100 orders. On the fourth day, I had to look 3–4 times to be sure and then call

Jeffrey to ask if those numbers were real. We had 1,200 orders in twenty-four hours. I just sat and watched the orders come.

Post launch, Harmon Brothers still cared. The technology changes every month, and Harmon Brothers knows this and keeps up on it. We got weekly calls from our account manager to help us adapt to algorithm changes, test new edits for various audiences, and rework the material into a social media friendly version.

Harmon Brothers is at the forefront of the market. With Orabrush, Poo~Pourri, our poop stool, and Chatbooks, Harmon Brothers has a way of finding and vetting the right company and culture, seeing if it's a match, and then making it happen. I felt they cared as much about *our* bottom line as their own—and they'd help us make key decisions with that in mind. Rather than just going for the short-term money, Harmon Brothers goes for long-term sustainability.

Bobby Edwards
Squatty Potty CEO

The unicorn changed the way we poop, and it changed our lives. It was frightening to trust Harmon Brothers with our reputation and our future, but it turned out their creativity produced a future beyond what we could have imagined. This book will show you how they did it, and how you might be able to do it too.

— *Bobby Edwards, Squatty Potty Founder*

Author's Note

I'm a long-time friend and admirer-from-a-distance of the Harmons. I also write books. So when the opportunity came to write a book about what they were doing, the ads they were creating, and—much more importantly—the company they were building, it seemed like a match made in literary heaven.

Yeah, well, it wasn't any heaven I ever heard of.

It was pretty great in a lot of ways, just not all of them. The Harmons couldn't have been nicer about letting me crawl through their lives. Writing is what writing is, and sometimes it's fun, and sometimes it's like scraping your chest with a cheese grater. But over the course of the three years as the book has been forming, the company—and I—have changed so much that writing a book about it felt a lot like trying to take a sharp picture of a kid in a bounce house while doing flips on a trampoline. Many, many days I was thoroughly glad I don't get motion sick.

A book like this probably doesn't need an author's note because it doesn't really have anything to do with me—I just get to write about what others have done. Still, I felt like some introduction was necessary. I've tried a preface, a prologue, a preamble, an introduction, an explanatory note to the text, and a partridge in a pear tree, and in the end, all I want to say is this:

It's been worth every second.

As an author, I write alone (I'm no HB scriptwriter, that's for sure). Being able to hang out with the Harmon Brothers as the company grew from a half dozen to just under thirty has been weird, and exhilarating, and fun. Sitting in the office, listening to the banter, and watching magic get made has made me almost feel like a part of it. I've been treated as well as I would have if I were one of the team.

Before you get to the good stuff, allow me to make sure one thing is absolutely clear: the principles I talk about here—they work. They aren't just talk. The Harmons, and the entire team that is part of Harmon Brothers, really believe in the principles that undergird the company, and they try very hard to act on them, every interaction, every day.

It was unexpected, but very welcome, to be a part of something larger than myself, even if for just a blink. I won't be the same again.

From everyone I talked to, everything I saw, I learned something valuable.

I hope you will too.

—*Chris Jones*

*To delve deeper into the Magic of Harmon Brothers beyond the scope of this book, go to **harmonbrothersbook.com/bonus** and watch free videos on their unique process.*

CHAPTER 1

IT STARTED WITH
POOP

{ *How did I become the author of this book?* }

One day, months before I was invited to write about Harmon Brothers, Theron Harmon walked down the stairs that separated our offices. Upstairs, Theron ran an advertising specialties business (and mined Bitcoin), and downstairs my team wrote mortgages while I wrote books. Though Theron and I had never directly worked together, we had been friends a long time. On his face was a look I'd seen before. It said, *"I need to tell you something, and I don't think you're going to believe a word of it."*

Theron Harmon
Client Happiness

"What's up?" I said, turning away from my laptop. Any excuse to stop writing will do. He slumped into one of my brown client chairs, facing away from my desk toward the wall. Out came a big sigh, and he rubbed his chin, trying to figure out how to begin. I waited. It always paid to wait, with Theron.

Me
The Author

"I've been talking with my brothers Jeffrey and Neal and Daniel. They're putting together a video ad for a client, and they have this crazy idea..."

He trailed off.

"Yes?"

He sat there a minute, mouth opening a little, then closing, as if he were trying statements out on his tongue to see how they tasted. Finally, he turned his head to me and said,

"What do unicorns poop?"

I'm a writer. People ask me weird things all the time. This, though, was right up there with the weirdest.

"Uh, I don't really . . . I mean, I don't write a lot about unicorns. I haven't given it much thought."

"But if you did."

Theron doesn't do small talk. When he asks you a question, he wants an answer. This mattered to him.

"Um, rainbows? Isn't that, like, a thing, rainbows and unicorns?" I said.

His mouth turned up at one corner, so I was partly right.

"And if you were going to serve rainbows to someone?"

"It hasn't come up."

"Seriously, what would you serve?"

I thought for a second. The payoff here was going to be something else, I could tell. And then I got it.

Sherbet?

I felt my way.

"Rainbow sherbet."

Theron sighed again, this time with evident relief, and a smile broke loose on his face. "I have a story to tell you. It involves a prince. And pooping unicorns. And rainbow sherbet."

And that was my introduction to the Harmon Brothers ad agency.

Theron's brothers had been making videos for a while, first for Orabrush, then for themselves, and now they'd landed a client that needed, um, an unusual way to advertise their product. That company was Squatty Potty. And the Harmon Brothers were about to go from interesting startup sideshow to one of the hottest ad agencies in the biz.

With unicorn poop.

Of course, it's much more than that. This is a story of perseverance, grit, innovation, and sometimes a little luck. And if you're saying to yourself, "Hey, I have all those things," then great, because the reason this book exists is so that others can do what the team at Harmon Brothers has done.

None of it is easy—few good things are—but the recipe for the Harmon Brothers' success is rooted in their culture, processes, and partnerships. These systems and principles will work for small business owners, company managers, startups, as well as marketing and advertising firms. Because in the end, what makes Harmon Brothers successful is not exclusive to them. The team at Harmon Brothers steadfastly insist they are not special. Anyone can do what they've done.

Let me warn you, though, the path is not lined with cheerleaders. People have insisted all along the Harmon Brothers' journey—

some are still doing it—that organizing a company this way cannot work for long. But this book shows that when the ice cream hits the fan, the systems kept churning away.

These same naysayers also balk at the lack of organizational structure and the diffusion of financial benefits to all parts of the company (see the Creative Culture section), at the loss of rigid institutional control (see the Creative Process section), and the

> **By the way,** Harmon Brothers has a podcast called "When the Ice Cream Hits the Fan" that's insightful and a lot of fun. You should check it out.

steps it takes to combine world-class products with world-class marketing (see the Creative Partnerships section).

And the way modern business has run these long years, you'll be tempted to agree with the critics. Selfishness, greed, outright theft—these are synonymous with big business in the twenty-first century (and if you take a look at history, you see these things all the way back to the pyramids). The Harmons are realists, not idealists, though they behave sometimes as if they were the most idealistic of people. What they've constructed is designed with real life in mind.

Their systems work not because they have perfect people at Harmon Brothers; but because they have systems designed to maximize the humanity of imperfect people.

These Harmon Brothers principles continue to function under the stress of interminable project delays, outright failures, and management reorganizations.

I've been in the room when things went sideways. It was then that this system showed its true strength.

But those stories come later.

CHAPTER 2

IN THE
BEGINNING

{ *Where the 3 C's of Creative Success begin.* }

The 3 Cs of the Harmon Brothers agency—Creative Culture, Creative Process, and Creative Partnerships— have their genesis all the way back before there was a Harmon Brothers, when there were just the actual Harmon *brothers*, three of the six—Neal, Daniel, and Jeffrey—and a cousin, Benton Crane.

At that point, there were no poop jokes, no unicorns, no rednecks driving cars off cliffs. Goldilocks had dropped no eggs. No mothers had jumped fully clothed into baths or been shot with crossbows. No soap opera stars had made out with their carpets (if you don't catch these references, they are all from successful ads Harmon Brothers had created by 2018). They had only barely begun to Share Better Stories (the phrase that would eventually become their motto).

All that, and much more, was still to come.

How did they get there?

Glad you asked.

It's Jeffrey's fault.

Jeffrey Harmon is the youngest of the three brothers in the group, is bald, and the one that started everyone else into making videos. His first video ad is used in business classes today because, according to Google (the company, not the search engine), his Orabrush ad was one of the very first videos commercializing a product on a global level using the YouTube platform.

Jeffrey Harmon
CoFounder

It started in 2009 when Jeffrey was in college at Brigham Young University (BYU). He had a business marketing class in which groups of students would assess various products to see if they had potential. On the last day of his senior year, Jeffrey sat in the back reading blogs on marketing.

One of the groups of students had taken on a marketing analysis project from a local entrepreneur. The product was a strange, low-tech gizmo that brushed gunk off your tongue as a way of controlling bad breath. The students had investigated it, looked at the marketing metrics, even performed a study of the market, and their conclusion: it would never sell online.

The inventor of the gizmo (now called the Orabrush) was a local biochemist and nutritionist, a man burdened with entrepreneurial spirit, who had this brainstorm and made a tongue brush, which he had been trying to sell for years. Literally, years. Obviously, he'd had very little success since he had—in some desperation—

reached out to the university's undergraduates for help in figuring out what to do with the thing. The man was Doctor Robert Wagstaff, and despite having a name fit for Hogwarts, everyone just called him "Dr. Bob."

Dr. Bob
Orabrush Founder

"I invented the brush in the early 2000s, though I'd had the idea for a long time. People's bad breath was so silly, really. It was obvious that most of the problem came from people's tongues. Cleaning that gunk off would make a huge difference. Even doing it with a tongue depressor, even their fingers, would help. But this brush was far better than those."

Dr. Bob is in his early 80s now, heavily gray, but still with a youthful twinkle in his eye and something in his face that is terrifically appealing. He's a man you want to be friends with, and not just because he has wonderful breath.

Dr. Bob: "We tried to sell the product locally to drugstores, but nobody wanted it. When we could get them to stock the product, it didn't make any difference. People just walked right past it. Finally, I got desperate enough to try an infomercial. I figured we couldn't do any worse."

Certainly there have been a small group of incredible success stories from doing infomercials. So Dr. Bob tried to join that exclusive circle. He went on TV to pitch the Orabrush, and then waited for the phone to ring and the product to take off. The investment to prepare the infomercial and pay for the airtime was a little over $40,000.

He sold 100 units.

And no, an Orabrush does not sell for $400 apiece.

The failure was crushing.

Dr. Bob: "It was almost despair that brought me to BYU. We tried everything we could think of and we got nowhere."

So he sat in a marketing class at the front of the room in the spring of 2009, and a college team of twenty-somethings poked holes in his idea.

Jeffrey: "They said that Dr. Bob should not try to sell it in stores or online, but that he needed to license the tech to a big megacorporation like Procter & Gamble. Their study showed that only 8 percent of people would buy a product like this online, so it wouldn't be worth it."

So of course, from the back of the room, Jeffrey raised his hand.

Jeffrey: "I basically said that I thought that was really stupid. Eight percent of people doesn't sound like a lot, but there are about two hundred million adults in the US, so that was like fourteen million people that would buy the brush online. I argued that selling it to those people was a lot easier than selling a patent to Procter & Gamble."

And then Jeffrey laughed. "They didn't really agree with me, and that was the end of it."

Except that it wasn't the end of it because after class, Dr. Bob sought out the kid in the back that pushed back on the negative review and asked him if he'd like to come work for him. Jeffrey already had a job lined up for the summer but said yes. He could work on it at night in his spare time, as a way to test some of his more avant-garde marketing ideas.

Jeffrey's research told him he should use social media to drive sales for Orabrush—only he didn't know how to do that because no one did. At that time, social media itself was just ten years old, and the only thing that ten-year-olds have ever been good at selling are Thin Mints.

In 2009, Facebook had just begun its takeover of the world (at a mere 140 million users), and at that time, only in the communications arena, not in business. There was as yet no YouTube integration or even any video posting. Facebook hadn't yet perfected wasting people's time.

So Jeffrey bought up a business Facebook page with a couple million fans for $5,000 of Dr. Bob's money and began to "market" to those people.

Jeffrey: "Basically, I just spammed the heck out of everyone. Facebook shut it down. But it didn't work anyway."

After a while, Dr. Bob came to Jeffrey and asked, "How much do I owe you?" because Jeffrey had been working for a few months and hadn't really been paid.

But Jeffrey responded, "I'm supposed to be getting this thing off the ground, and I'm not doing that, so you don't owe me anything."

Dr. Bob didn't like that answer, so he took Jeffrey out back of his house and showed him this two-year-old motorcycle he had. It was the only thing he had to give him. And Dr. Bob was tired of driving car-less Jeffrey back and forth to meetings, so win-win.

Jeffrey: "It actually turned out to be a good trade because I didn't have a vehicle anymore, and I didn't want to buy another car until I was out of debt. So I took the motorcycle as payment for my work. But by the end of the year, things had changed."

Devin Graham
Videographer

Knowing that he had to switch to something more catchy than social media spam, Jeffrey hired a fast-talking, charismatic pitchman named Austin Craig and put him in front of the camera to talk about the unique qualities of the Orabrush tongue cleaner. He grabbed his roommate, Devin Graham, to do camerawork and another roommate, Joel Ackerman, to help write the script.

The video is low budget, and the sound isn't great.

Jeffrey: "We shot it in a pool hall we rented out for two hours. Austin was late because he's always late, and by the end, they had reopened. If you listen close, you can hear the pool balls clacking in the background." There's a cheap joke to be made here, but I will move on.

There isn't anything about this story that tells you it's the beginning of something revolutionary.

Jeffrey's day job was to manage a group of twelve social media interns at FamilyLink.com. Austin was on Jeffrey's team while Jeffrey was noodling the first Orabrush

Cameraman Devin Graham has now skyrocketed to fame and fortune as a filmmaker, with multiple lucrative YouTube channels and Facebook Watch pages (he's known as Devinsupertramp—you and several million of your closest friends may have heard of him or at least watched his adventure and extreme sport videos). But at the time, he was Jeffrey's roommate and a film student at BYU—he was just starting out. He used an entry-level camera to film the Orabrush commercial. And Jeffrey was lucky to have him.

video. Austin would come rolling in (late) and launch into political rants about the issues of the day. Crowds would gather because he was passionate and hilarious. Jeffrey thought he'd be a perfect pitchman for the video. He was.

Austin: "I really didn't think it would amount to anything, but Jeff offered me $100. I had just graduated from college (so had Jeff) and that kind of money meant something to me at the time. Jeff was also wickedly intense about everything, and he was putting a good team together. It looked like it would be fun to be a part of. Anyway, we shot the video on a Friday, and it was pretty cheap, but I had fun with it."

They spent $500 on the ad, shot it all in a weekend, and went to see *Wolverine* at the dollar movie theater as soon as they were done. Then they edited and worked on it until it released a month later.

Austin: "Then it just didn't stop growing. The ad, I mean, I thought it was just fun. It wasn't going anywhere. But Jeff knew how to test it, how to push it. My friends at work would stop by my desk and say, 'Hey, did you see? Your video has a 1,000 views.' And then it was 10,000. And 50,000. And 100,000. And then it just went crazy."

YouTube had just launched what would become its most successful ad format, TrueView, which gave viewers the option to choose the ads they want to watch. Previous to this launch, the YouTube team had flown out to Provo to meet with Jeffrey and he helped them figure out how TrueView should work. Jeffrey was at the forefront of advertising on YouTube.

Jeffrey: "By our own estimates, we were buying about 90 percent of YouTube's inventory in the early days. It was hard to miss the ad back then. We were advertising almost exclusively on YouTube. Naturally, Google was thrilled to see us regularly spending on its video platform."

A million dollars' worth of tongue cleaners were sold online a year after the video launch. Consumers began asking their local retailers to carry the tongue cleaner in their stores and uploading their own reviews of the product on YouTube.

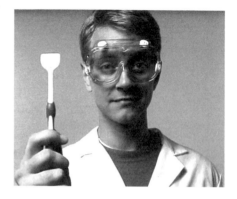

Jeffrey: "Orabrush went on to be stocked on store shelves in twenty-five countries, and the majority of our international retail partnerships came when retailers called us because they were being bombarded by shopper requests. It showed us the reach and impact of YouTube."

Jeffrey brought in two of his brothers to join him at Orabrush because if nepotism were a punishable crime in Provo, Utah, nobody would be able to staff a company. Neal Harmon's job started as technical—his intense work ethic and programming skills are brilliant (he almost got carpal tunnel)—but he ended up as a top leader in the company, which isn't unusual for Neal. Daniel Harmon, who never met a creative project he didn't want to tinker with—you should see the LEGO sets on his desk— headed up Orabrush's script writing and video production. Together, the three of them planted the seeds of the current Harmon Brothers system.

Although just beginning, the Creative Culture (with a people-first culture and an innovative compensation model), Creative Process (successfully combining creativity with productivity), and Creative Partnerships (albeit with just the one company so far) were finding soil and taking root.

——————————— ———————————

PART 1

CREATIVE CULTURE

{ *What is it that makes people want to work, not just go to work?* }

FROM POOP TO GOLD

CHAPTER 3

POO~ POURRI

{ *In which the HB culture reports for doo-ty.* }

It's 2013, and the Harmon Brothers crew is filming on a set created to look like the inside of an office restroom. Actor Bethany Woodruff is in a blue semiformal dress, sitting on a toilet framed by utilitarian bathroom stalls. With a posh British accent, Bethany follows the sound of a flushing toilet with the line, "You would not believe the motherload I just dropped." Thus begins the commercial for a product called Poo~Pourri. And the director is trying to figure out how to keep the crew from laughing during the shoot. It's messing up the sound.

Poo~Pourri, a pre-pooping spray that prevents toilet odors, is clearly not Orabrush. What happened to Orabrush?

The short story is that Orabrush management changed, conflicts emerged, and when Poo~Pourri began aggressively recruiting them, Jeffrey and Neal shifted their focus from slaying bad breath to slaying poop stink—same kind of work, from the other end, if you see what I mean.

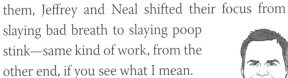

They wanted their brother Daniel to make the switch too.

Daniel was working as a graphic designer in Chicago when his two brothers brought him to work for Orabrush. He describes himself as "a typeface nerd." He's the tallest of the three, well over six feet, with dark hair and blue eyes. He's devilishly handsome and the envy of every man in whatever room he's in. Yes, Daniel told me to write that. And yes, then Daniel told me to *remove* that. But I only follow instructions so well.

The brothers are close, right back to their days growing up in Idaho, weeding beets, irrigating potatoes, and playing in the canal that ran along not far from their place. Their combined sales experiences included selling alarm systems, potatoes, cows, school snacks, and window-washing services.

But when Neal and Jeffrey left for Poo~Pourri, Daniel remained working at Orabrush full time. He did, however, help with the Poo~Pourri script and in editing the video. Partway through this process, he decided to go all in, and he turned in his two weeks' notice at Orabrush.

Jeffrey recruited their cousin as well.

Benton Crane, the soon-to-be operations guru at HB, grew up in Utah but spent summers in Idaho with the Harmons. His methodical knack for channelling creativity into practical logistics was just what the Harmons needed.

When Jeffrey invited Benton to join them, Benton was intrigued. With post-college experience in Washington DC, he was, at the time, a consultant at Deloitte. And Deloitte had treated him well. Very well. He'd have to be insane to leave a job that good. But he'd been following what they'd been doing at Orabrush. What was the new company and product?

Poo~Pourri. A poop spray.

It sounds kind of silly when you just say it out straight, but . . . well, no, it *is* silly. Only it works. The stuff really does eliminate odors from pooping.

Over the past few years the company's sales had been good, but Poo~Pourri wanted something more, and they figured that if Jeffrey and Neal could sell a product that fights bad breath, they could also sell one that eliminates odors from the other end. They pitched it to the Harmons, flying them to Hawaii to discuss it and sending emails like,

"Do you like talking about poo? This isn't a spam; well it kind of is but hear me out . . . I'm obsessed with your marketing skills— seriously blown away (just did a guru bow on the plane to you)."

The Harmons agreed to take a crack at it.

Taking a crack at it would require a whole team.

But sometimes Fortuna calls your name and you have to leap. Benton wanted in. He joined the team as the video distribution arm, buying ads and doing video optimization.

Neal, Jeffrey, and Daniel had done a good deal of market research and testing at Orabrush, and they knew they could move product off the shelf if they pitched the video correctly. Harmon Brothers had, in other words, a model:

- Outline the problem
- Make the product the solution

- Add in some calls to action
- Lay on the humor

And now you've got an ad that sells. It should be a cinch, right?

The biggest problem was that humans dislike talking about their bodily functions, to the point that in almost every language on earth, one of the worst swear words you can use has to do with feces. Poop is as taboo as $#!@.

Most commercials advertising bathroom products stay well away from any actual representation of the reason the bathroom is there in the first place, which ain't the bath. Heck, the word *bathroom* gets used in place of *toilet* even at tiny highway rest stops, where there isn't a bath for miles. Harmon Brothers could have gone that way, sticking with the madding crowd, but they had another idea and the guts to run with it.

What if, instead of avoiding the issue, they gave the tail the same treatment they gave the tongue? What if they went 180 degrees from the rest of the industry and laced the entire script with as much crap as possible?

Joel Ackerman (Jeffrey's former roommate) was the main writer on the script.

Joel: "I kept putting more and more poop references into it, and every time I thought, 'This one goes too far. They're never going to go for it,' and every time Jeffrey would say, 'That's awesome. More.' So I put in more."

He included this thesaurus of poop metaphors: "So whether you need to pinch a loaf at work, cut a rope at a party, or lay a brick at your boyfriend's, your days of embarrassing smells, or prairie dogging it, are over."

The script called for a blue-gown dressed, classy young lady to talk brazenly about defecation, or rather how to neutralize the stench in the first place. It needed the right face, but more than that, it required a great performance. And a British accent.

Daniel: "We don't usually know who we want to cast until we do the auditions, but once we see the right person, we know."

In this case, the right person was actor Bethany Woodruff. They insisted on her even in the face of determined opposition from the client.

Jeffrey: "They took some convincing. They thought Bethany wasn't right for the role."

The client had pictured a traditional sporty magazine supermodel, and Bethany didn't fit their picture.

To their credit, once filming started (the entire thing, from script to launch, was done in six weeks), Poo~Pourri realized there was something truly

English Accents make things funnier to Americans. Ask John Cleese. Or you could ask the Government Employees Insurance Company (GEICO). In 1999, GEICO wanted to do an ad, but because of a Hollywood actors strike, they couldn't get anyone to go on camera. The solution was an animated character complaining that people can't get his name right because of the massive demand for GEICO, a company not very many people had heard of at that point. But they did hear of it later, obviously, and the Gecko (after the first two ads, sporting an English accent) has become one of the most recognizable characters in advertising history. GEICO has grown from a little under $5 billion to a bit over $20 billion over that period. All because of an English accent? Maybe.

special happening with this ad. The director, Joel, kept having to cut because the extras were laughing. And the camera crew. And pretty soon a whole bunch of other people.

They went out of the gate with six video variations. The idea was to test them with unlisted links on YouTube, watch the statistics on each to figure out how well they worked, and determine which converted (which turned watchers into buyers) the best. Normally it takes two weeks to gather the data. But by the first weekend, whether Harmon Brothers would've picked it or not, *The Huffington Post* blogged about one of the variations, so that was the variation they had to go live with. And it went viral.

Ironically, the viral version wasn't even the best-performing of the tested group. There were variations that did better—and are doing better still today. They convert better and have more views.

Daniel: "The title we landed on— "Girls Don't Poop"—actually didn't come from us. It wasn't one of our ideas. It came from commenters on YouTube, saying 'No way, girls don't poop.'"

> **An unlisted link** on YouTube means a video that isn't searchable but that anyone with the link (or who is fed the ad) can watch. It's a great way to quietly A/B test which ad is the best before a public launch.

Benton: "We tested it, of course, and it turned out wildly effective."

The public-facing video has 40 million views, but the unlisted ones have 45 million or more. Getting picked up by the press was a very good thing in terms of a launch, but it destroyed the strategy of picking the best-performing ad and making that one the public face.

"*Huffington Post* got it," Jeffrey said, "and there we went."

If this is the worst problem you have, you're probably doing okay. Although its popularity did create problems of its own.

Daniel: "The ad blew Poo~Pourri up beyond their wildest dreams. They could not keep up with the inventory. They told us that they were set up to handle the traffic, and after the ad exploded, it turned out there were not nearly enough bottles of Poo~Pourri in this world."

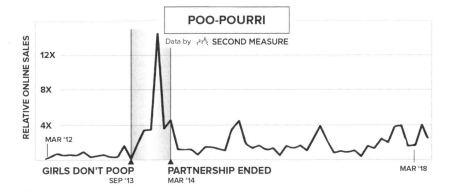

The ad went viral on YouTube and got shared all over Facebook. It further cemented and proved the model that had begun at Orabrush. Still, the last thing on their minds at that point was starting an ad agency.

Benton: "When Poo~Pourri went to cut the check they asked Jeff, 'Who should I write this to?' and Jeff and Neal looked at each other (this was at eleven o'clock at night) and Jeff says, 'Let's just call it Harmon Brothers; we'll change it later.'"

Daniel: "So Neal jumped online and registered Harmon Brothers LLC; they wrote the check, and next thing we know, *Adweek* picked up the Poo~Pourri ad and cited *Creative Agency: Harmon Brothers*, and we all looked at each other and asked, 'Are we an agency? I guess we're an agency.'"

Benton: "It literally wasn't on our minds in that way. We were just trying to make a campaign for Poo~Pourri. The intent at the time was to have a partnership where we would become part of Poo~Pourri in the same way Jeffrey, Neal, and Daniel were part of Orabrush. And it turned out that business-wise that didn't work out. And then it had run all over the press that we were Harmon Brothers, and the name stuck. So here we are, Harmon Brothers, branding experts who didn't even decide our own name."

At this point, Harmon Brothers was growing more into what it would become. They had a name, albeit accidentally. They'd added a second viral campaign to their reputation, showing that they could at least do it twice. And their creative culture was solidifying.

So what is the Creative Culture that makes Harmon Brothers so special? What have they found that allows them to retain a creative, free-flowing environment while churning out some of the most successful and most decorated client work in the industry? How do they maintain such a low rate of turnover, which runs counter to their industry?

Well, let me show you what it looks like when you walk in the door.

Once Katie Camillett, the office manager, lets us in the door to Harmon Brothers Headquarters, here's what we see:

Jonah Rindlisbacher clicks away at an iMac. His blonde cowlick swoops to the right like a Nike symbol. He sits in a swiveling chair, black and chrome, with armrests. His station today is the middle row of what looks a great deal like the bridge of the starship Enterprise (and is actually called that), with two unbroken ranks of curving desks lined with computer equipment. Action figures, model spacecraft, combat drones, and LEGO creations are littered here and there like nerdy confetti. Jonah is transferring files from one massive multi-terabyte drive to another even more massive one. It's tedious. In between uploads, he's tapping on his phone.

Jonah Rindlisbacher
Line Producer

There is no one else in sight because everyone else is on a shoot. It's a Tuesday morning, about ten, but Harmon Brothers feels empty.

Around the bridge of the Enterprise, four ready rooms (yep, that's what they call them) are arrayed. Their doors do not make a *shush* and slide open when you approach, which is admittedly a little disappointing.

Another door leads to a small kitchenette and then to another very large workspace, this one with tables, lined with chairs. A small conference room opens off this space, occupied by Theron Harmon.

Theron is the eldest Harmon brother and was brought on to help with "Client Happiness" (a real HB title) in 2014. His greying sideburns and diplomatic mild manner help Harmon Brothers navigate the shoals of strong personalities. Now the Growth Team Lead, he's pacing back and forth as he talks energetically on his cell.

Off in the dim distance, Katie sits at a strategically placed desk, keeping an eye on a glass-walled conference room complete with a flat-screen monitor the size of a Smart car. Power access strips sprout from the desks and floor, daring anyone to spill a drink.

At one table, Jonny Vance types on his laptop. He's an almost impossibly cheerful man, with a kooky sense of humor he claims was honed while trying to make his stoic father laugh. Jonny's working on a script of some sort and he's redone one of the lines six times in the last two minutes. Clearly making laughter is work. No one else is here.

Correction. Tyler Stevens arrives. He smiles and heads back to the bridge of the Enterprise, flops down into one of the chairs, and fires up his Mac. On screen is a shot from a video for an upcoming launch. Settling into his headphones, he runs through five to six seconds of video, pauses, and does it again. And again. Video editing is Groundhog's Day in microcosm.

Tyler turns to Jonah.

"Is Kaitlin here?"

Jonah pulls one earphone off.

"Coming in this afternoon, she said."

They put their headphones back in place and work goes on.

Throughout the day, people come and go, with no discernible schedule.

It's early afternoon and Kaitlin Snow Seamons walks in with her signature yellow beanie and bright presence to match. She takes up a place along the second bank of monitors on the bridge, making a cozy three-party meeting. They chat about delivery schedules, video rendering times, and other things arcane enough that reproducing them here would be impossible. The meeting happens right out in the open, where anyone could walk by. People do. They are occasionally consulted about something but most often not.

Mike Henderson, officially titled Video Omnivore, which is the HB version of jack-of-all-trades, floats into place on the bridge, puts a couple terabytes of media onto one of the hard drives, and motors off down the hall.

Daniel Harmon and Benton Crane arrive. They've been out on the shoot and are just checking in before they head back out again.

This is a moment of truth—when the cat is away, the mice will play, the saying goes. The mice don't appear to have been playing, exactly, except for the spirited conversation about Star Wars dueling drones, but surely when the bosses arrive the work level will ratchet up significantly. Less texting, at least. Something.

There is no discernible change in attitude. The conversation— Star Wars still the topic and plot holes in sci-fi movies as a whole—does not pause.

Jonah: "Daniel, Benton, I'm glad you're here. Can we talk about Save the Storks?"

Save the Storks is a nonprofit company Harmon Brothers are producing a hero ad for ("Hero ad" is Harmon-speak for a big, full-length ad). Up to this point, every video had pitched a specific product, but this video solicits donations to an organization that provides free ultrasounds to pregnant women. This project is different. Harmon Brothers has never done an ad that explicitly asks for donations. As with the first time anyone does anything, the process is . . . developing. All six of the assembled staff, loosely grouped together, have things to say. All opinions are considered.

The discussion has to do with a fairly serious matter—whether the hero ad they're planning to shoot actually fits the client, or whether they have fundamentally misunderstood the reality of the Save the Storks business model. This perspective threatens to overturn three months of work. Tens of thousands of dollars ride on the results of this conversation.

It is impossible to accurately describe how thoroughly weird this scene is for someone who has spent decades in traditional business.

Jonah has become a significant player at Harmon Brothers over the last year, but he is a walk-on—literally—to the company. He came to Harmon Brothers as a wannabe actor, auditioning for the part of the prince in the Squatty Potty video, and when he knew he wouldn't get it, asked if there was something—anything—else he could do, like sweeping floors, scrubbing toilets, dust-bustering the Enterprise, etc. Three years later, he now does more or less anything and everything, including, apparently, serious creative meetings that could make or break a whole client piece.

Significantly, you would not be able to tell the difference between the founders and the walk-on from the tone of the meeting, who is listened to, or from what is said, or by whom.

Everyone has a take. Opinions fly—and these people are far from shy about expressing them. All the while, off to one side, Mike is working on photos. He's not part of this discussion, but no one seems troubled that he will hear it. He, himself, is blithe as a butterfly, doing his thing while an apparently haphazard group of people make decisions about a half-million-dollar project ten feet away.

Opinions are stated with authority and confidence, but not heat. At Harmon Brothers, anyone can say anything, no idea is blatantly disregarded, and no one takes offense when their idea is rejected. The discussion ranges widely, and a decision is made and delegated, and everyone goes back to doing what they were doing before. The meeting takes at most half an hour. Kaitlin waves goodbye and goes out. Benton and Daniel head back to the shoot.

Making a rare appearance at Headquarters are the two Bretts, Brett Crockett and Brett Stubbs. They sit for an hour in the

Brett Crockett
Funnel Team Lead / Designer

Brett Stubbs
Tech Lead

open desk area, drawing things on paper and pointing at their screens. They both normally work remotely, but sometimes you need a face-to-face to unknot difficult website issues.

There are no Ping-Pong tables here, no foosball, no free drink machines (though the fridge is full of some sort of craft energy drink from a potential client, with a note begging people to try some and leave feedback). Neither, however, are there time clocks or even personal offices.

Every work space is inhabitable by anyone for any length of time. Dave Sullivan has spent most of the afternoon in ready rooms, soaking up sun and working on spreadsheets of some kind. When he leaves, the room is empty. It's not his. It's *theirs*, all of theirs. Well, technically it's still Dave's for another twenty-two minutes because he really ripped one in there.

David Sullivan
Finanace Director

Culture is not entirely atmosphere, but all of atmosphere is culture. American culture is hamburgers and hip-hop, texting and traffic jams, football and Facebook—not because someone designed it that way, but because that's what's in the air. Those things work together to create what people think of as "America" today.

Similarly, the walk through Harmon Brothers Headquarters shows the atmosphere at HB. The building was designed for cooperation and collaboration. The attitude from all levels and titles shows that input is welcome no matter the source. There's trust in each other that the work will get finished on time with high quality, even if they're talking about drones right this second. Where does a culture that encourages such creative freedom come from?

Some of it comes from the upbringing of the founders and leaders of the company, their loose, almost Tom Sawyer-like home life.

Some of it is the millennial ethos of the place—the average age here cannot be above thirty-two, and when I'm not in the room it's probably twenty-seven—tempered with an old-school work ethic that sees sixty-hour workweeks as nothing unusual if there's a shoot going on or an imminent ad launch.

Some of it is design—the layout of the building with its mid-century modern, minimalist décor, and combination of private and common areas.

And some is happy accident—like ubiquitous Wi-Fi that makes doing creative video work possible on a laptop anywhere in the world (there are some full-time HB team members that work entirely from home).

It is easier to see the fruits of the culture than condense its definition into one sentence. And one of the fruits is found in employee satisfaction.

Those who don't abide this very self-responsible culture and ultramodern workflow do not stick with the company long. And those who do stick around thrive.

> **The Harmons' home life** was complete with self-built treehouses, zip lines, and a raft with a sail. Neal Harmon even talks about having gotten some of those ideas from The Adventures of Tom Sawyer, Mark Twain's classic novel. Neal: "I thought I hated to read, and then Mom gave me a book, and I read it, and she gave me another one, and I read that, and after a week straight I discovered that I loved reading. I spent a lot of time with Frederick Douglass and Tom Sawyer and other books like that. They gave me ideas."

The amount of turnover is small, especially for a firm so young, so close to the founding, and so wildly successful. And most of those who leave continue to collaborate and maintain connections to the company. Success attracts, like moths to the lamp.

As *Mad Men* reveals, the advertising industry is high stress, high pressure, known to cause failed marriages and visits to heart surgeons. Nevertheless, when there is stress (and it does happen), the Harmon Brothers culture makes it worth it through hiring the right people and allowing people to dictate their own schedules.

Abe Niederhauser
Lead Media Buyer

The ad industry is also typically cutthroat, get-your-own-at-all-costs. Yet one of Harmon Brothers' core stories is how Abe Niederhauser, king of HB ad spend analytics, on one particular project was paid substantially more than he was due and not only caught the error, but paid the money back even though his employee contract was a handshake.

American business is typically closed, opaque, and secretive. Yet Harmon Brothers has creative decision-making meetings in an open-access 30x40 room with no walls or soundproofing.

If this were a Roald Dahl story, Slugworth wouldn't need to bribe Veruca Salt to steal one of Willy Wonka's Everlasting Gobstoppers.

Abe Niederhauser is one of those who has now left Harmon Brothers. But he deserves mention not only because of his amazing ad-buying skills, but because of his exit—he became successful investing in cryptocurrency and decided to go see the world. Harmon Brothers is hoping this is just a creative sabbatical and that he'll return at some point, full to the brim with innovative ideas. It probably depends on the crypto prices.

He could walk in and grab a whole box of the candy. Because you can steal products. But you can't steal the culture that created them; you need to create your own. You *can*, however, read a cookbook, like the one you're holding in your hands.

Culture is life to a business. "Changing the culture" is a mantra thrown around by nearly every wobbly firm from Silicon Valley to Wall Street. Ordinarily, this means, "We have to become a good place to work, or it's going to cost us millions to retain our people." Harmon Brothers, though, pays a bit less than top dollar up front, yet still has a list of people wanting to join the company.

They know culture and how to bake it.

But the proof of the pudding is in the eating. So if the pudding looks good, smells good, but sends you to the ER with food poisoning, that's not ideal. Let's put this tasty recipe in the oven with Harmon Brothers' most memorable ad and see if it's still delicious.

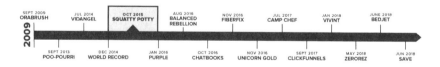

| SEPT 2009 | JUL 2014 | OCT 2015 | AUG 2016 | NOV 2016 | JUL 2017 | JAN 2018 | JUNE 2018 |
| ORABRUSH | VIDANGEL | SQUATTY POTTY | BALANCED REBELLION | FIBERFIX | CAMP CHEF | VIVINT | BEDJET |

2009

| SEPT 2013 | DEC 2014 | JAN 2016 | OCT 2016 | NOV 2016 | SEPT 2017 | MAY 2018 | JUN 2018 |
| POO-POURRI | WORLD RECORD | PURPLE | CHATBOOKS | UNICORN GOLD | CLICKFUNNELS | ZEROREZ | SAVE |

CHAPTER 5

SQUATTY POTTY

{ *In which a creative culture risks it all
on a wackadoodle unicorn.* }

I t's 2015, and I am on Squatty Potty's set, watching a mystical unicorn puppet…poop. The puppet is cute and cuddly and ends up triggering an international fad for unicorn plushies and t-shirts. Today it sits on a toilet, squats its little hooves on a white stool, and demonstrates how to unkink a colon. Apparently it solves a problem for a lot of people—it will have more than a quarter-million shares in its first month of launch.

But how did they get here?

After Poo~Pourri's successful ad, Harmon Brothers also finished an ad for VidAngel (it involved shooting paintballs at a family dressed in white) and one for the Radiant Foundation (which broke a world's record for Largest Live Nativity in the World). While these ads performed extremely well, Harmon Brothers still didn't have consistent clientele to keep them busy.

Enter Squatty Potty, a small company in St. George, Utah, that already had solid success from being featured on the hit ABC show *Shark Tank* a few months before, but they wanted to take their company to the next level.

Squatty Potty had an interesting but quirky product—a stool that raised a person's knees when they sat down on the toilet so that they would sit in a squat, rather than the unnatural (if common) position western toilets put poopers in.

Squatty Potty had seen Harmon Brothers' work on similar products and thought they might be a fit for their own. But initial negotiations did not go well. One big investor didn't think Harmon Brothers had anything to offer, and if they did, they should offer it for free. That was a nonstarter.

Eventually, Squatty Potty CEO, Bobby Edwards, gave HB the go-ahead (go back and read the foreword if you missed it). It was October when the hero ad was ready.

And what an ad.

Most products for feces elimination use soft euphemisms or don't even refer to the act of defecating at all. A popular toilet paper brand uses cartoon bears who talk vaguely of "comfort." On top of that, a quick Google search reveals that bears don't even *use* toilet paper.

Harmon Brothers decided to flip the script.

Suppose for a second that unicorns pooped.

What would that look like?

Ice cream, of course. But not just any ice cream, no. Rainbow sherbet (with or without glitter and sprinkles). So for the Squatty Potty ad, instead of avoiding the part where the pooping happens,

Harmon Brothers put it up close, in your face, and had little children eat it in cones.

Edgy? Yeah. You could say that. Or maybe delicious—once you get past the gag reflex.

A pooping unicorn is a mammoth of a risk to take with an already established brand. But Bobby Edwards and company were one of those rarest of animals: a small business on the ground and a big media mindset. They really do believe that their mission is to change the way the world poops.

Bobby's mother, Squatty Potty founder Judy Edwards, might not have been entirely persuaded that the unicorn was the way to go, but she has missionary fire in her eyes about the Squatty Potty device. Judy once suffered from colon and digestive problems and points out that people spend billions trying to rectify bowel issues that could be solved by this very simple, very inexpensive "stool for better stools."

They could have soft-grown to be much bigger than they were, a little at a time. But they didn't want to do that. And when they said they wanted to go big and launch for the moon, they actually meant what they said, with everyone's *moons* in mind.

Wes Tolman
Prince of Poop

The video itself took a couple months to get into shape. The narrator is a handsome student from an acting school in Florida named Wes Tolman. He channeled everyone from Aragorn to Captain Jack Sparrow, keeping a (mostly) straight face while spitting out lines like, "Can't get the last scoop out of the carton?" and "The Squatty Potty gives you a smooth stream of fro-yo that glides like a virgin swan."

And worse. Really.

Judy says, in a post-launch interview, "It was like three days before launch, and at that point you're so close to it you don't know if it's good, if it's bad . . . I was scared. I was nervous of what this was going to do to our brand, and how people were going to perceive this crazy, wackadoodle unicorn."

Jeffrey and fellow team member Derral Eves, HB executive producer for this project, were point men for distribution. But as luck would have it, on launch day they were in Poland, speaking at a conference.

Jeffrey: "We got the video uploaded to us and tried to get it up on the web while we were driving down the highway in Poland, bouncing from crappy hotspot to crappy hotspot. We did finally get it uploaded, in the middle of the night."

It was still daytime in the States, though (hooray seven-hour time difference), which was plenty of time for things to get seriously out of control.

Jeffrey: "I logged back on and we had something like two million views already. I thought the counter was malfunctioning for a bit. But it kept going up."

And up. Four million. Five. Six.

"This Unicorn Changed The Way I Poop" racked up *eight million views in the first twenty-four hours.*

In the first week, internet searches of Squatty Potty were up 600 percent. And then the orders started rolling in. Retail sales quadrupled.

Internet sales exploded to six times the previous volume. It's a radical idea to make your spokesman a faux-English prince backed by a pooping unicorn, but radical is the only way to get results like this—and a culture of creative freedom can get radical

The successful launch, understandably, converted the skeptical investor as well as the board. Bobby and Judy Edwards were overjoyed at the success of the project. They poured money into the video, pushing it into a newly available advertising channel: Facebook.

Up to this point, YouTube had been by far the most profitable way to get exposure for Harmon Brothers' hero ads. But with this launch, Facebook had just initiated in-line video playing, where Facebookers could see the videos on their wall and watch them without having to leave the site.

Jeffrey: "This was the first time that Facebook's views exceeded YouTube's. Our conversion rates from the videos started going up on that platform. They've been better ever since. Facebook is currently the place those videos get seen."

Retail sold out. The warehouses shipped their back-stored product. Then that ran out. The manufacturing ramped up to maximum, twenty-four hours a day. And then those were gone as well. By Christmas, the ad sold Squatty Potties out of every retail establishment in the country and backordered them on the internet as well. By the time the "Beyond the Shark" follow-up episode finally aired, there were literally no available Squatty Potties anywhere in the US. The ad had blown past the boost from the *Shark Tank* appearance four times over.

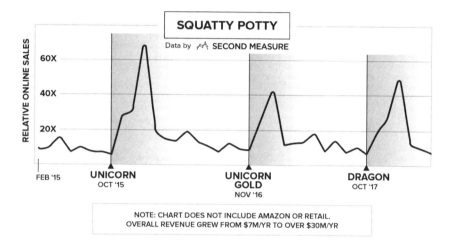

Harmon Brothers found new ways to talk about poop, and people listened.

This video was risky. It required a Creative Culture that embraces innovation and empowers its people to make decisions. So maybe it's time to explain how Harmon Brothers creates this culture.

Find out how to choose a central idea
as iconic as the pooping unicorn by going to
harmonbrothersbook.com/bonus

CHAPTER 6
....

**BUT REALLY,
HOW DOES HB CREATE THIS
CREATIVE CULTURE?**

Harmon Brothers is a place people want to be. The culture makes it so—because a successful culture is not just the people, but also the systems. And HB's systems maximize productivity *and* the humanity of imperfect people. Both together allow the company to churn out hit after hit. And *systems* can be imitated—maybe even by your company.

Here are nine parts of the current system that support Harmon Brothers' culture of flexibility and innovation:

1. Hire the Right People

Harmon Brothers hires people who figure stuff out. That skill set enables them to look at the big picture and determine what to do to make an impact.

When Mandy Shepherd was in her hiring interview, Benton Crane asked, "What is your life mission?" She didn't have to think about it. She said, "To create beauty and educate the ignorant." She is now directing/producing high production-value education courses for Harmon Brothers University (master class episodes where Harmon Brothers shares their secrets for making ads that sell—for more, see the back of the book), living her life mission within her job.

One of the ways Harmon Brothers is able to maintain such a unique culture is by hiring the right people—and they don't do this by looking at a résumé and asking where you attended college.

Benton: "When I set up a job interview with Mandy, she had done a couple ads on her own, and I already knew she was capable. I was planning on hiring in a role where I wouldn't manage her. So what I really wanted to uncover was how our company WHY aligned with her personal WHY.

Benton Crane
CEO

She may have been the only person I've interviewed who actually knew her WHY. And the moment she shared it, I immediately saw that she could help us fulfill our purpose, while we could help her fulfill her purpose. I was no longer worried with work style or anything because we were aligned to the same mission."

The life mission question helps connect Harmon Brothers with people who can thrive in a culture of creative freedom and trust. It's why people don't just clock in at HB. They feel like their productivity matters, both personally and professionally.

Asking for stories rather than simple answers has also become a core part of Harmon Brothers interviews.

This terminology, looking for a person's WHY, comes from one of Harmon Brothers' core books—*Start With Why* by Simon Sinek. Instead of asking someone what they're doing or how they're doing it—if you really want to uncover the essence of a person—look for why they do what they do. Sinek's premise is that we can find much greater fulfillment by making our actions consistent with our internal WHY. Why? You'll have to read the book.

Benton: "Instead of a direct question like, 'How do you handle stress?' I'll ask, 'Tell me about an experience where you were under stress.' I just want to hear their story as a backdoor into what I'm looking for."

Benton also starts the job interview by describing Harmon Brothers and their mission to Share Better Stories.

Benton: "I watch carefully for their reaction as I talk. For some, it looks like what I'm saying goes in one ear and out the other. I take that as a sign that they're not connecting with what Harmon Brothers is all about."

Those applicants end up searching elsewhere for work.

Unusually, job interviews occur *after* a testing period. A person to be hired is often brought on first as an independent contractor to work on a specific project, or sometimes as an intern. If the team likes the person's work, cultural fit, and attitude, then they can be hired on a more permanent basis.

Jake Christensen was an intern for a shockingly brief time of three months and is now a member of the HB Funnel team. In his official job interview post internship, Benton was explaining the Harmon Brothers mission when he saw the fire welling up inside of him.

Harmon Brothers has four teams: Admin, Creative, Funnel, and Growth. Admin handles administration. Creative creates content. Funnel distributes the content. Growth lands and handles clients.

Jake later said, "It's kind of amazing. I thought I wanted to come to Harmon Brothers to learn their tactics so I could use these tactics on my life mission. Instead, I realized I could fulfill my life mission by working *at* Harmon Brothers."

What makes this even more interesting is that Benton didn't even have a specific job for Jake. But by the end of that interview, Benton was remembering the saying, 'Put the right people on the bus and then find them a seat.' "I didn't know what kind of work Jake would end up doing, but I knew he belonged on the bus."

A culture that depends on trust and has an overwhelming number of moving parts works best with employees that share the same ideals.

2. Test Ideas in a Laboratory

Most of Harmon Brothers' hero ads contain a test of some sort. Data is convincing. And the testing occurs in the research phase (to decide if the product is a good fit for HB), in the pre-shoot phase (to visibly demonstrate for an audience why the product is better than the rest), as well as after the video is finished and launched (to conclude which ad variation is the most successful).

> ## This "bus" phrase
> belongs to Jim Collins, who wrote it as a principle in one of the best-selling business books of all time, *Good to Great.* The book is about how some companies go from small to giant industry leaders and others don't. According to Jim, finding seats for the right people is one tip to taking your company to greatness.

But the testing doesn't stop there. Harmon Brothers also has a special meeting called the Hypo Lab (short for HYPOthesis LABoratory) which is a weekly meeting where people can bring up any new product, system, idea, or structure, from the smallest tweaks to major refocusing of the company mission. No idea is too wacky for the initial brainstorm list.

The lab idea sprang from what Benton calls his worst mistake while leading Harmon Brothers.

As we've mentioned a couple of times throughout this tale, Harmon Brothers likes business books and often takes nuggets of wisdom from them to improve their culture and systems. This time, however, that was an error.

Benton: "The mistake was when we based one full year off philosophy from the book, *Essentialism*, by Greg McKeown. (*Dear Greg, I personally love your book. It just didn't work at Harmon Brothers. Please do not savage me on Goodreads*). We had had a couple big successes and were buried in companies wanting to get our attention. Trying to figure out which leads to take was eating up all our time and focus. So we read *Essentialism,* which made the argument that we should only answer the question, 'What makes you world class?' and then just do that."

Harmon Brothers management concluded that they were world class at long-form conversion ads. They had the pattern down and decided that these ads would give them the greatest chances of success.

Benton: "What I failed to realize is that innovating beyond where we are already at is *also* essential. And sometimes to innovate beyond what we are good at, we have to say yes to projects that are trying something new but might not have as high a probability of success. Looking back, we didn't innovate at all that year. We got stale. And our copycats closed the gap that year too."

Recognizing that innovation is vital, they needed a system to encourage constant innovation and trying new things. Enter the Hypo Lab. The intent of the lab is that anyone throughout the whole company can brainstorm an idea to the hypothesis list.

Then they meet (anyone in the company can participate as a tester), look over the list, and decide which hypotheses to test. A minimum of two and a maximum of eight ideas start out on the list, but usually only one or two make the cut for that week. After selecting one hypothesis, they figure out how to test it and what resources the test will require. They gather the data and lay out the results. Most ideas don't test out, but even those are far from a waste of time. Week by week, Harmon Brothers is building a repository of ideas and research.

Another purpose of the Hypo Lab is to challenge the Harmon Brothers team.

Benton: "We used to be pretty tight-lipped about how we do what we do, but we are changing to openness and transparency. As we tell the world our secrets, our team is challenged to go do something new to stay ahead."

You can steal the system—heck, you're holding a manual in your hand—but you can't steal the culture that makes that system work. Take what they're doing now and use it. Their goal is to already be on to the next thing.

One of the ideas that passed the test of the Hypo Lab is to try and make a musical ad. This is the new golden age of musicals, after all, with the incandescent success of *La La Land, The Greatest Showman,* and *Hamilton* just in the last few years. Harmon Brothers has never attempted one before. Keep an eye out.

A culture based on innovation needs a "lab" to create and test ideas.

3. Add Wisdom to Meetings

Monday morning at Harmon Brothers features an All Hands meeting. One deeply held belief at Harmon Brothers is that good ideas come from anywhere, and in order to maximize the chance of those ideas, all team members are expected at this meeting every Monday.

In the beginning, Harmon Brothers meetings happened with whoever was there, with little structure—the company was small enough and the projects few enough that word would get around well enough. Over the last couple of years, the company has grown to the point that it's impossible for everyone to know and understand what their colleagues are working on. The All Hands meeting fixes that.

Each team leader gives a brief, high-level report of what they accomplished in the week prior and then what they plan to accomplish in the coming week. Not only does this give context and visibility to the work everyone is doing, it also provides a forum where ideas and solutions can come from anywhere (e.g., an editor on the Creative team might suggest a solution to a problem that is plaguing the Admin team).

Furthermore, 5–15 minutes of the meeting is set aside for a Moment of Wisdom. The giving of a Moment of Wisdom is rotated, and the speaker gives a presentation on one of their passions or hobbies (they toyed with the idea of calling it a Moment of Passion, but on second thought, that sounded like a romance novel). Most of the time the topic is not work related—electric cars, Dungeons & Dragons, documentaries, censorship politics, or nutrition to mention a few. Not only do Moments of Wisdom build team unity, as people get to know things they never would've known about each other, but it also keeps the team learning about subjects beyond their work.

A flexible culture needs people who can freely exchange ideas and who think beyond their own cog in the wheel.

4. Give People Creative Space

Not all meetings are for work topics, but all the meetings *are* clustered on one day: Monday from 8:30 to 12:30. After the meetings finish, the entire company gathers for a catered lunch. Everyone is encouraged to break away from work to eat and mingle. Sometimes impromptu games come up. The atmosphere is loose. It allows the team to get to know one another on a personal level, which greases the wheels for the high-stress work to come.

It should be pointed out again that this is the last official meeting *of the week* at Harmon Brothers. All the team meetings, department meetings, even meetings like the team lunch, are packed into Monday before real work starts. It's important to keep those meetings from interrupting the flow of work and breaking the creative focus. Compressing the time frame also forces the meetings to be conducted at warp speed and with maximum efficiency.

Team relationships are vital in a culture so balanced on trust, and a culture that has meetings only one day a week is a culture of happiness.

5. Trust Your People

At Harmon Brothers there are no mandatory hours.

Tiffani Barth
Project Manager

This creative freedom is one of the things that lured Tiffani Barth to Harmon Brothers in 2016, hired from another local ad agency. But before that job, she worked in LA on a TV show. "When I worked in Hollywood, I was expected to work twelve-hour days, whether I needed to or not, and was penalized if I didn't. I even got calls at 4 a.m., with my boss demanding me to respond immediately. It was such a culture of fear. Harmon Brothers upsets this industry. People in Hollywood say, 'If you don't have thick skin, then you don't belong here,' as if we really couldn't create anything better for ourselves. But Harmon Brothers says, 'We value your abilities and trust you to manage yourself.'"

At Harmon Brothers, people come and go to work at will. They can work long nights or early mornings, or leave for the day at lunchtime. They might work at home the whole week. They might work three eighty-hour weeks on a project, and then take a week or two off to relax. People keep track of their own hours and contributions, incentivized to do so because of the bonus structure (see Chapter 8). And that incentive, plus hiring the right people, is how the team can trust each other to get the work done.

If you want teenagers to take a long time to mow the lawn, pay them by the hour rather than the job. This holds true for adults too. To minimize the likelihood of time card bloat, Harmon Brothers compensation is mainly project oriented, not time oriented.

This does, admittedly, sometimes lead to hard, difficult work and temporarily long hours. On the recent Zerorez launch, a short conversation with the client about recording voice-overs turned into a grueling all-night rework of the entire ad. This was ten days before launch. But it needed to be done for the ad to be maximally successful (see more details on the Zerorez story later).

A culture where change is constant needs people who accomplish projects and overcome obstacles, rather than people who punch out at 5:00 p.m. whether they've solved the problem or not.

6. Make Time to Focus

Many companies see the value of a retreat, where employees gather at a comfortable location and eat delicious food and talk about projects and get trained. While Harmon Brothers' retreats do include a posh location and tasty catering, each retreat has only one specific purpose.

One example is the HB Writers' Retreat, with the purpose to choose a script for the hero ad. The writing team presents several scripts, and then the writers, client, and HB team hammer out the best ideas from each script into one.

Harmon Brothers also holds a Partner Retreat, where the top management discusses the company goals for the year (it was one of these Partner Retreats that developed the company WHY of Share Better Stories).

Whatever the retreat, Harmon Brothers always has *one* specific objective to accomplish at the retreat.

Plus, they have a "no phone" rule in order to strip away distractions. Use your phone, no matter how short the call, and it'll cost you (usually $20, which goes in a pot and is raffled off at the end to a participant who didn't use their phone). The lack of outside contact is a feature, not a bug, and allows the team to focus on mapping a path to the one goal.

An innovative and flexible culture benefits from concentrated time together accomplishing a specific goal.

7. Be Ready to Change

Recently Harmon Brothers held an Operations Retreat to examine their systems in detail. A number of "hotspots" had developed over the preceding few months, and employee surveys had shown that a few features of the Harmon Brothers culture—things like loose organizational structure and lack of written contracts—had begun to generate negative feedback loops. People sometimes didn't know what their responsibilities were or to whom they should report.

It was possible that Harmon Brothers needed to grow again, but without a systematic way of assessing the jobs to be done vs. personnel cycles, it was hard to know for sure.

What happens when your business needs collide with your culture?

....

There is a difference between culture as principle and culture as tradition.

Sometimes the culture as tradition (e.g., no defined organizational chart) conflicts with the culture as principle (e.g., do excellent work and don't burn out your people).

Harmon Brothers holds regular assessment meetings in which they take a look at cultural system artifacts and try to decide what is beneficial and what is not—what is principle and what is not. If it does not help Harmon Brothers Share Better Stories, it needs to go.

The key here is that Harmon Brothers—and your company will not be any different—does business a certain way. Some of that will be good, and some of it certainly will be bad.

To have inefficient, wasteful, even dangerous pieces of company culture isn't the kiss of death. What *is* the kiss of death is to become so wedded to "this is just how we do things here" that you're unwilling to change them when it becomes clear those things are holding the company back.

Harmon Brothers is willing to change. It's a hallmark of the culture. That also means that, to an extent, the company culture is constantly evolving. By the time you read this, some things will undoubtedly be different. You should probably buy every future edition of this book, just in case.

8. Celebrate the Successes

This is an area in which Harmon Brothers, to be perfectly honest, has been up and down. In the beginning, client launches were celebrated with parties. Signing a new client was an occasion for bursting into song. But over time, as the company grew, those celebrations seemed superfluous.

They aren't. Celebrating wins is a critical part of a healthy culture.

Recognizing this, Benton instituted a quarterly celebration to celebrate everything from the preceding quarter (birthdays, engagements, anniversaries, new hires, new clients, campaign launches, etc.). At the celebration's dinner, they list the successes and give everyone a chance to applaud them. Then they watch a movie because they are definitely movie people.

Since it takes long hours and all-nighters to finish most of the Harmon Brothers projects, acknowledging that dedication also reinforces the hard work part of the culture. On one occasion, all the team members who worked all-nighters to finish a project were taken to Topgolf to celebrate.

Celebrating successes together helps make positivity part of a company culture and is not only fun, it encourages dedication. Right now I am treating myself to a full sleeve of Oreos because I finished writing a whole page today.

9. Only Work on Projects You Are Passionate About

Harmon Brothers carefully agrees to advertise *only* a product they feel passionate about. This is an unusual part of their culture. They don't take on a project just for the money, no matter how much it is.

Outsiders frequently comment on how unique it is that they turn away would-be clients—even clients ready and willing to write a large check. Whatever the product, before contract negotiations, samples are tried by as many of the team as possible. They have to like it. They have to feel *passionate* about liking it.

Adhering to this principle means that before production even starts, the team members are already enthusiastic fans of the product. That energy not only makes a higher quality ad, but is another reason people stay late and overcome obstacles on behalf of the client.

If you're thinking that being passionate about every project is a luxury only smaller companies can afford, you're right. In fact, Harmon Brothers has made a conscious decision to remain small precisely *because* they don't want to have to take a paycheck for a project they don't believe in.

The standard model for an ad agency is to grow headcount and client count as aggressively as possible, and it is true that doing that can lead to massive profits.

But the byproduct of that is that it forces you to take on clients for whom you have no passion. It forces you to take on employees who might not align with your WHY. Harmon Brothers decided (in a Partners Retreat, actually) to go the other way.

Benton: "Staying small allows us to be selective about who we work with, who we hire—selective about when and how we work. For the client, it guarantees that they get the best of the best creative talent—guarantees they get our passion; they get our focus. Ultimately it gives the client a higher probability of a successful campaign."

A culture that demands passionate work must remain choosy about the work it does—even if that means sacrificing profits on the altar of making sure every launch is awesome.

The nine items above are far from an exhaustive list, and being willing to change sometimes means that one or another of the nine gets modified.

Harmon Brothers is not a perfect place. But it is relentless about its culture and Sharing Better Stories. That won't work if the story of each team member isn't a happy one.

But suppose those stories *are* happy? People are satisfied with their job. Is that enough? Sure, if you think an AMC Pacer is a fine car.

Let's see if we can't put something more exciting on the track, something with a nitrous oxide boost. Nitrous, in this case, is called passion, and when you add it to the happiness already in the tank, let me show you what kind of horsepower you can get.

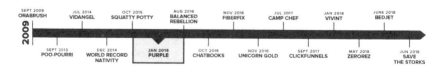

FROM POOP TO GOLD

CHAPTER 7

PURPLE MATTRESS

{ *In which much testing reveals a culture that is just right.* }

It's December 2015, and I'm on a set built right in the Purple mattress factory in Alpine, Utah. Actor Mallory Everton is dressed as Goldilocks, bed expert. She tries a mattress. It's too hard. In a development no one could ever guess, the next one she tries is too soft. Will the Purple mattress be just right? Oh, the agony of suspense!

The suspense isn't the problem. The problem is how to *demonstrate* the just-rightness of the mattress. But then Mallory yanks a cord, and a glass panel with eggs secured to the underside plummet downward. Below them, their destination: a Purple mattress. Impact.

The eggs remain intact and the whole room erupts in cheers. Mallory throws herself onto the glass and bounces up and down. Still none of the eggs break. Goldilocks pronounces the bed just right—then she is eaten by a family of bears returning from a walk in the forest. But the crew has the shot, so it's okay (no, that is not how the ad goes).

Until 2014, Purple, then known as WonderGel, made seat cushions and licensed their cushion technology to other manufacturers, including a couple mattress companies.

The factory is in Utah—not exactly the middle of the manufacturing belt of the US. It's not even in Salt Lake or Ogden, which at least have a traditional manufacturing base. It's in Alpine, and although that sounds like a sleepy ski resort town, it isn't. Alpine is a bedroom community on the wrong side of the Rockies for any significant snow.

After seeing the success of the Harmon Brothers' videos for Poo~Pourri, the brass at Purple thought their company might be ready to move out from the shadows to make a splash of their own. Who better to advertise an obscure mattress manufacturer than the guys that made poop products cool?

But marketing-wise, this was a different sort of challenge. For a poop spray, or a toilet stool, or even a tongue brush, the challenge was getting people to try something they'd never tried before. That wasn't the problem here. Instead, it was getting people to switch from something they already had to something better. It was demonstrating that this new, rather unique Purple mattress was enough of an upgrade to be worth the hassle and expense of replacing their old familiar one.

Jeffrey: "Squatty Potty was a brand-new market. Poo~Pourri was a brand-new market. Orabrush was a brand-new market.

Purple, though, was a different concept. For one thing, it was far more scalable than anything we'd done before. I thought Orabrush was a big market because there was eight percent of the population that would buy it. But a hundred percent of the population sleeps. It's a multibillion dollar market."

First, though, the Harmon Brothers team had to sleep on it.

Jeffrey: "I had been looking for a good mattress anyway. I'd slept on some good ones before, and I knew they were pretty expensive but totally worth it. My brothers, though, man, they were sleeping on boards."

But the Purple beds were not quite ready for prime time yet. All through the fall of 2015, while HB was working on the Squatty Potty ad, they were trying out Purple's beds. A lot of work still had to be done to get the mattresses ready to disrupt the market.

Starting with the name and logo.

Theron Harmon: "When Tony and Terry Pearce approached us, the company wasn't called Purple. Their retail brand was WonderGel. One of the first things we had to deal with was the name of the company. Tony, the CEO, conceived the name Purple. It's a brilliant name and the material could easily be dyed that color. We all agreed the name had that 'empty vessel' quality, into which you could pour meaning."

Daniel Harmon: "The simplicity of it was appealing. After more than a month of discussions and design iterations, I finally got the logo right and we came up with the tagline 'No Pressure, It's Purple.'"

When building a brand, Harmon Brothers starts with one or two syllables that don't carry a lot of semantic baggage.

The next thing was the bed.

Daniel: "Tony and Terry are true scientists. They had tested scores of prototypes. They had this sandwich design, with a light layer of foam on the top and foundation layers of foam on the bottom. The patented Purple material lay just beneath the thin top layer. But ultimately we all agreed that the mattress needed to showcase the proprietary material, not bury it."

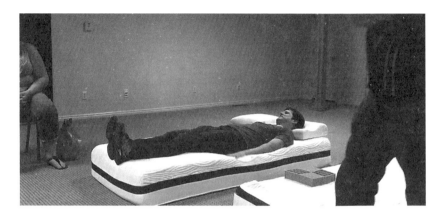

Jeffrey: "After trying many different foams, we finally put the Purple material on top of the mattress. At first everyone was hesitant to do it because we were worried that people didn't like the feel of the gel grid, but, in the end, that was exactly what people needed to feel." The last part of the redesign was the mattress cover. Before any changes, its colors were light blue and white, with a botanical pattern. Jeffrey hated it, and the feelings across both teams were mixed. Tony and Terry invited Harmon Brothers to collaborate on a new design. And Daniel Harmon and Brett Crockett were honored with naming credits on the design patent for the cover (at that time, Brett Crockett was HB's graphic designer; he is now their Funnel Team Lead). Everyone at Purple and Harmon Brothers loved the finished product. It was a marvel of comfort engineering. Finally, the bed was ready for hard-core sleeping.

Jeffrey: "I knew Purple finally had a good mattress when I stopped going to the chiropractor. My back used to go out every couple of months unless I was actively exercising, and then I started sleeping on the Purple and it never happened again. That was when I knew this was something special."

And Jeffrey hasn't exercised since. Okay he has. But he doesn't have to for back pain.

The HB team received the final version of the redesigned bed and tested it for themselves. Conclusion: They loved it. The next step was designing a campaign unlike anything they'd done before.

Humor would be a part of it, definitely, because this is Harmon Brothers. But due to the cost difference, it couldn't be aimed at the same demographic and be successful. It would need to appeal to an older crowd. There's a good-sized difference between five bucks for a tongue brush and a thousand dollars for a mattress. Clearly impulse, on-the-spot purchases were not going to be the key drivers of success here.

But how to demonstrate that this mattress was better than all the others? Something visual, compelling, obvious, featuring someone that knows about beds?

Of course it starred Goldilocks— the closest thing to a bed-comfort expert you can get—extolling the virtues of the bed and even testing it using raw eggs. But that raw egg test was one of the most difficult parts of the entire ad.

To demonstrate the remarkable properties of Purple's seat cushions, made with the same material as the mattress, the company had been using a raw chicken egg. They would place it on the cushion, and have people sit on it. The egg wouldn't break.

Daniel: "In fact, I couldn't even really feel it, which just told me how terrific this material was."

The original script had the egg test with the seat cushion as the demonstration of value. But it sucked on film. "Kinda looked like someone *laid* an egg, actually," one observer said.

Harmon Brothers tested all kinds of things.

Benton Crane: "Early on, it became clear we had to do something with glass, so you could see it. We went to a gym and stacked weights on a glass sheet, with eggs underneath. That worked, but the visual was bad."

Benton Crane
CEO

The glass could hold 1,200 pounds of weights before any of the eggs broke. That's a fearsome pile of weights, but it doesn't do much on film. Weights are not very charismatic actors.

And then, the breakthrough. On Jeffrey's suggestion, Benton attached the raw eggs to the underside of a thick sheet of plate glass, then suspended the eggy panel above the mattress. A solution! But it was extremely heavy. And the actor needed to drop the glass with a simple tug. Luckily Terry and Benton figured it out—just forty-eight hours prior to the shoot.

It gave them the visual comparison they wanted. The egg drop broke eggs on every mattress they tried. Except Purple's.

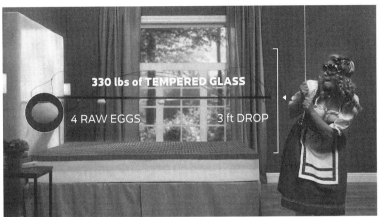

330 lbs of **TEMPERED GLASS**

4 RAW EGGS

3 ft DROP

While working on the demonstration test, they were also auditioning for the right Goldilocks. Dave Vance, when writing the script, had a Studio C actor in mind, the versatile Mallory Everton.

Dave Vance
Lead Writer

Daniel: "We auditioned over 200 actors in person and online, but we came right back to Mallory in the end. She had just the perfect blend of humor and

Studio C is named, appropriately enough, for a studio at Brigham Young University's television station BYUtv (available on most cable and satellite networks). It's a sketch comedy show in the Second City/Saturday Night Live tradition. As BYUtv's most-watched show, several sketches have launched some members of the team into modest stardom, including Matt Meese, whose Scott Sterling sketches have been viewed millions of times worldwide. Writers from the show have worked for Harmon Brothers from the beginning, and several of the actors have appeared in HB hero ads.

heart. She slept on a Purple mattress for three months before we started shooting, so she believed in it, and you can tell."

Shooting finished and the postproduction timeline was tight. But less than two weeks before launch, the web development  contractors doubled their price. Paying this would have blown up the rest of the budget. In a scramble, a longtime friend of several Harmon brothers, Brett Stubbs, rescued the project. He is a full stack software engineer, a genius really, and after pulling multiple all-nighters, he built the site within the original budget and did it in a week (Brett Stubbs joined Harmon Brothers full time after that).

The video went live in January of 2016. Once again, as in both Poo~Pourri and Squatty Potty launches, production could not keep up with orders. Purple sold out. Backorders reached six months.

The Purple commercial continues to air, now at almost 400 million views and when Purple went public, it was valued at over $500 million.

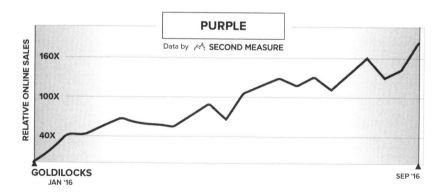

FROM POOP TO GOLD

If you can do it once, that's nice. When you do it twice, people pay attention. But when you do it three times—Poo~Pourri, Squatty Potty, and Purple—you've got something. What was it

Interestingly, it didn't seem to hurt the brand that people had to wait—people will wait a good while for a truly outstanding night's sleep. There is actually research on this—people value things they have to wait for. Acquiring something instantly is great fun (and addictive, thank you, Amazon), but for something special, the anticipation is part of the enjoyment. Think of Christmas here—counting down slowly increases the impact of the day itself. Haunted houses (to cite just one example) have learned that people are more satisfied with the experience if they have to wait before entering (about twenty minutes is optimal). They will sometimes even hold people at the front gate so they can get that anticipation working, even when the place isn't busy. I once ran a haunted house. We may or may not have done this. Purple certainly didn't make people wait on purpose, but it didn't kill the business when people had to wait as long as six months for their beds to be delivered. It was worth it, and they knew it would be.

that let Harmon Brothers hit three straight home runs (other than the obvious advantage of working with companies that have a P in their name)?

Like Goldilocks' original fairy tale where she tests the porridge, the chairs, and finally the mattresses, testing was essential to the entire Purple ad campaign. Goldilocks is the original testing scientist—she could have been an employee at

Mallory Everton
Goldilocks

Harmon Brothers. Harmon Brothers helped test Purple to prepare it for market. They tested different demonstrations of the product to hone in on the strongest story. They tested machines to build the egg drop test. Testing is fundamental to the culture at Harmon Brothers because it is the recipe that brews creative magic.Speaking of brewing, no matter how much you test, normally when you create a culture that hands people this much autonomy, what you're brewing is *trouble*. Is there a way to keep the freedom of yeasty action without blowing up the vat?

There most certainly is. Wanna know how?

CHAPTER 8

A SUCCESSFUL
CREATIVE PROCESS
BALANCES BOTH SIDES

It's 2016, early spring in Provo, Utah, home base of Harmon Brothers. Fluffy April clouds drift by overhead. Neal Harmon eats his savory breakfast pastry on an outside patio and thinks.

Neal Harmon
CoFounder

Neal: "We don't like managing people. We think people manage themselves, and they will, as long as you design the incentives properly."

After a conversation with an investor about a startup that was experimenting with merit-based profit sharing, Neal and Jeffrey implemented a similar system at Orabrush. Now at Harmon Brothers a few years later, they were polishing it. They recognized that a Creative Culture needs a system that channels creativity toward completing a project—and a carrot always motivates better than a stick.

Their compensation model mirrors the sort of company the Harmons have always gravitated toward—flat structure, no rigid hierarchies, lots of democratic input, and a reliance on adult behavior without pages of rules. But would it work as the company grew?

At the time of this conversation, Harmon Brothers had done well over the previous few months with the successes of hero ads for Squatty Potty and Purple. Often the most dangerous time in a company's life is when it goes from no money to a little bit of money.

How would the model hold up? Forecasts said things would be fine.

We all know about the problem with forecasts.

Jeffrey Harmon
CoFounder

A couple of weeks later, I'm at breakfast with Jeffrey Harmon, who is as responsible as anyone for the unique compensation model at Harmon Brothers. He's sipping a juice, sitting on a barstool, tapping something into his phone.

Jeffrey: "Sharing the money is smarter. There's more for everyone. We make sure the bills are covered and share out the rest."

It sounds counterintuitive, but multiple studies have indicated that poor people share their nothing much more readily than rich people share their plenty. A quick survey of VH-1 documentaries is sufficient to show that most bands do just fine until someone starts handing them money, at which point they blow it all up. The systems that were fine for one- and two-man shops often fail under the stress of expansion.

Me
The Author

Me: "Is that not dangerous? Not keeping more of the profits in the company?"

Jeffrey: "It's a lot more dangerous to lose the best people in the industry. The people are what make Harmon Brothers work. There's always more money. But how do you replace the people?"

Focusing on the people at the company, and not simply on the profits, allows a unique culture to develop. It also saves money, which seems counterintuitive, since the compensation package involves sacrificing money on the altar of keeping good people around. But if the resultant pie is bigger, everyone wins, except for the guy who hates pie, because this pie is made out of cash. Most companies talk about win-win scenarios with their employees, but very few actively design systems that prove they believe in them.

Radical Idea: The company should take 50 percent of its profits and split them with all the creators that made them possible.

How is that compensation even possible? This unique compensation is part of the Harmon Brothers' secret sauce. Here are some of the ingredients necessary:

Flexibility

It would have to be flexible so that the differing demands of various projects would fit the model without substantial alteration—whether a project required fifteen people or fifty, the model would still work.

Measurability

It would require that projects be quantifiable in terms of dollars generated for the company so that rewards could be accurately shared without having Peter rob Paul.

Control

It would give control over distribution of the rewards to the people that earned them, instead of management—a bottom-up approach where those most directly involved in the work of the production would have the greatest control over the sharing out of the rewards for it.

Trust

It would also require a great deal of trust on the part of management, trust that the employees involved would not use their increased influence over compensation to harm the other members of the team, or to unfairly enrich themselves.

....

The secret sauce to this Innovative Compensation plan has four necessary ingredients: *Flexibility, Measurability, Control,* and *Trust.*

It may seem that such a system cannot exist, or that if it can, it would require more than is possible to expect from a modern workforce. But this is precisely the system the Harmons experimented with at Orabrush, and when they founded Harmon Brothers, they updated and improved on the concept. It's a bedrock system in their company.

The more local and immediate a reward is, the more impact it will have on behavior.

Here's a simple example: If I ask you to put in two hours a day building an ice cream stand and promise you that if you do that, when the stand becomes successful a couple of years from now, you can get a cone every day if you like, that might be attractive to you. But if I told you that as soon as you were done building the basics of the stand, you could have one ice cream every day we made a profit, how much better and faster would you work? How much more tightly focused would you be on doing productive work to get the stand to profitability?

That's the model.

And here's how it works at Harmon Brothers:

At Harmon Brothers, incoming revenue is determined by two factors: up-front fees and ongoing advertising spending.

Each person who works on a project gets paid a minimum amount (often a little below market value), but then they're bonused based on their contribution to completing the project successfully. And these bonuses are where the compensation gets motivating.

Another way of saying "completing a project" is "solving a problem." And problems come in two varieties: well-defined and ill-defined.

Most compensation programs are based on well-defined problems. But creative projects often have ill-defined problems. This is especially apparent on a project like Squatty Potty. How do you advertise a stool for propping up your feet while you poop? How do you build an animatronic pooping unicorn? How do you figure out what demographic to pitch that to? Do you pay the unicorn in cash or pixie dust?

How can a company plan for every contingency, and reflect variable compensation, with any possible hope of getting it right—especially months beforehand when staffing for the project?

**Successfully completing projects
(a.k.a. solving ill-defined problems)
is why compensation at Harmon Brothers
is tied to contribution—not anticipated
contribution but observed contribution.**

Observed contribution to the project is measured not only by the management, but by everyone that participates in the project itself. Your *peers* determine what percentage of the rewards belong to you. These are the people working alongside you, not some HR wonk at corporate in Alpharetta. Titles mean nothing. Job descriptions mean nothing. Your pay level or management title entitles you to nothing. This part of the compensation is specifically merit based.

Make no mistake. Everyone gets paid for their work.

There are four core teams at Harmon Brothers: Admin, Funnel, Growth, and Creative.

The first team, Admin, has ongoing work, so most are paid traditionally, hourly or salary.

The second team, Funnel, are bonused on ad spend (the amount the client spends to promote the video). And the last two teams, Growth and Creative, have people who work on a specific project, and the bonus can be worth more—potentially *far* more—than the billable hour sheet.

These teams are the ones who benefit from this unique bonus structure: After expenses are taken into account (hard costs, salaries, rent, LEGO decorations for the office, etc.), **HALF of**

Harmon Brothers' remaining profits are allocated as a bonus to the internal team members that worked that project.

Half. You read that right.

That's 50 percent of both the remaining contract amount for the project and 50 percent of the ad spend *for as long as that lasts*. As clients continually spend money on ad promotion, everyone that worked on the ad gets paid for it.

Compensation for the ad is divided into three phases, and that 50-percent bonus is allocated in thirds among the three phases:

Phase One: Client Acquisition

Phase Two: Script Writing

Phase Three: Ad Production

There is some personnel overlap in the three phases (and like anything in the Harmon Brothers, there are current discussions to test other models). But for the most part, people tend to collect around one phase or another; although, they are not permanently locked to any phase. It is not unusual to have Harmon Brothers team members try their hand at different roles within a phase, or even to work on two different phases in the same project.

Either way, the 50-percent bonus is allocated in thirds among the three phases. Phase One team gets one-third. Phase Two team gets one-third. And Phase Three team gets one-third. Let's outline this with round numbers, so it's easy to see:

Project Contract: $1,000,000

Hard Costs: $700,000

Total Profit: $300,000

50% Allocation: $150,000

Phase One Team Bonus: $50,000 (1/3 of the allocation)

Phase Two Team Bonus: $50,000

Phase Three Team Bonus: $50,000

That's a $50,000 bonus per phase team. If you worked on more than one phase, you could dip into more than one pool. The tangible rewards, as you can see, are potentially quite substantial.

Additionally, the percentage of allocation among the team members is determined by the team members themselves.

This is done by that great American tradition: plunder.

Just kidding, it's done by vote.

Upon completion of a particular phase, a Google Sheet (another great American tradition) lists everyone from the core team who materially participated in the project.

Each team member has a week to put into the form what their contribution to the project was as they see it (often called a "brag session"). At the end of this week, each member receives a certain number of "shares"—an equal number for each team member—and has a couple days to allocate those shares.

None may be allocated to oneself. All of them have to be given out to others. And they are given as you see fit, based on the value your peers brought to the project.

The results are tabulated by a neutral third party, and an allocation percentage is determined based on these popular voted shares. The pot—in the example on the left, $50,000—is distributed to each member of the team according to that percentage, and that money is paid out as a bonus.

This doesn't happen just once, of course. Every month, the client has the opportunity to spend additional money with Harmon Brothers to promote the created ad.

The more they spend, the more goes out to the team that produced the ad, in a continuing royalty.

Often, clients will spend tens of thousands of dollars for the Harmon Brothers team to continue to work their magic. How can a company afford such a large ad spend?

··

Companies will spend on ads that bring in more money than they cost.

It would make fiscal sense that a dollar of advertising spend is supposed to generate more than a dollar of sales. In the traditional ad game, especially with high-visibility advertising (looking at you, Super Bowl commercials), it does not, at least not right away. But Harmon Brothers target a higher than dollar-for-dollar ratio, if at all possible.

This high of a return ratio also means more ad spend which creates more revenue which creates more ad spend—it's like your own personal money printer, but without the felony. Or so the ClickFunnels ad says (we'll get to the ClickFunnels story later).

The back-end compensation, thus, dwarfs the money made in billable hours—as long as those hours were productive and judged to be so by the team. There isn't any hiding. The team knows who is and who is not pulling their weight. Sucking up to the C-suite will cut no ice. Their votes do not count any more than anyone else's (though they do get to vote, as long as they contributed to the phase work). In fact, sucking up to anyone might lose you votes, Benton says, so people just don't do it.

What this also means is that no Harmon Brothers team member is going to slack off on a project. Not only would that cut their individual compensation, but it cuts the compensation for the entire team. The better the ad is, the more successful it is—the more the team will make, not just now, but in perpetuity. A rising tide lifts all boats, and the Harmon Brothers team are all on their boats, sailing into the sunset.

Everyone wins. Everyone makes money. Repeat.

....

**The client's success is the largest
determiner of compensation for the team.**

You work as much as you like, as well as you can, and you're compensated directly for that effort. It's the perfect blend.

Kaitlin Snow Seamons: "I love the compensation structure. I like how this structure motivates you to do your best work because you know you'll be judged by your peers. I notice who works hard and how committed and invested they are, no matter what it takes. And I vote them more shares."

If you see something that would be great to do, something that might add to the overall success of the ad, there's no need to ask if the extra hours can be added to a paycheck down the road. The model takes that into consideration, and that extra work will be recognized and rewarded. The incentives are still powerful and perfectly motivating to the task at hand: work hard to Share Better Stories.

A compensation model that rewards good work is a powerful way to boost morale in the workplace.

The Harmon Brothers' compensation model is an integral part of the Creative Culture of the company. And this Creative Culture is how Harmon Brothers team members can work so hard, doing meticulous, often exhausting work, over long periods, with an eye for the smallest detail and no tolerance for anything short of excellence. The culture naturally motivates people to do their best work.

PART 2
······················

CREATIVE
PROCESS

$\left\{ \begin{array}{l} \textit{How do you create a rigid framework} \\ \textit{for process that liberates the creativity?} \end{array} \right\}$

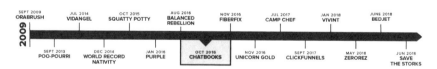

FROM POOP TO GOLD

CHAPTER 9

CHATBOOKS

{ *In which Harmon Brothers'*
creative process drips with authenticity. }

It's summer in 2016, on the set of the Chatbooks ad. Across a wide expanse of studio floor stands a huge bathtub, custom-built to be at least three times the size of a regular tub. Yes, you should be so lucky. Actor Lisa Valentine Clark lies up to her neck in bubbles, smiling, relaxed, and then in one motion, like Venus stepping from the waves, she's standing. "Do you think I have time for a bath? I'm fully clothed."

The contrast between the graceful movement and the blunt comment gets laughs, which is the point, but behind the laughs are a couple of engineers high-fiving. A surprisingly difficult scene has been smoothly created by an invisible piece of movie magic.

For a human to rise up out of the tub in a graceful way is physically impossible. Try it. You feel like a walrus. You look like one too. When you're in a lying position, to get up quickly and safely and smoothly just can't happen. Humans have knees.

We need help, something between a forklift and a crane. Or in this case, a levered platform underneath.

Daniel Harmon
Chief Creative Director

Daniel: "We built a custom tub that was 3x as deep as a regular tub, raised on a set built up roughly head high. Lisa isn't lying down; she's crouching. When the moment comes, she stands up, and the riser keeps her balance from tipping backward. It gives her momentum and her legs do the rest."

You don't think of it—much less see it—when you watch the ad, which is the point. She needs to stand up, but *we* need to concentrate on what she's saying, not what she's doing.

And what she is talking about is a product called Chatbooks.

The idea behind Chatbooks is very simple: everyone likes to take pictures. But having your life on your phone—or even online—isn't nearly as satisfying as having a book you can pull off the shelf (plus having your five-year-old drop a book into the toilet is way less expensive than your smartphone).

But making such a book—scrapbooking, as a previous generation called it—takes a long time and a lot of work. As the Chatbooks Mom character says, "Now there's a solution that I do have time for, because it takes no time." The Chatbooks service does the photo booking for you, automatically. Hook up the service, post your usual blizzard of photos on social media of your super-adorable children doing their super-adorable things, and a hardback book of memories shows up at your door.

No, seriously.

Vanessa Quigley, founder of Chatbooks, and her husband Nate have seven children. "I used to scrapbook, make photo albums, but as life got crazier I kept taking photos, but I wasn't doing anything with them. I wasn't even printing them. My youngest got to be six and I realized I didn't have a single physical photo of him. Anywhere. Chatbooks was founded to solve that problem for busy moms like me."

Harmon Brothers didn't expect virality from the Chatbooks ad. The plan was to target ads at likely customers and incrementally build an audience for the product. It didn't work that way at all.

Right out of the gate the ad produced a massive share rate and went viral so fast *it paid for the entire ad campaign in forty-eight hours.*

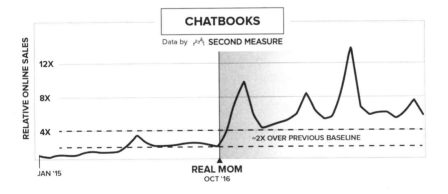

Daniel: "It way exceeded our expectations. We knew it would be a good sales tool, but we had no idea it would go viral to that degree."

As it happened, I got to see this one from outside mission control. I was out of town at a family reunion when the video launched, and the first I heard of it was my sister—who has six children—demanding that all of us gather around her 5.75-inch phone screen to watch this hilarious new video. We had to watch it four times, because the first three I couldn't hear anything over the gales of laughter from my sisters.

....

This ad connected to women all over the world. Not only because it was funny, but because it felt like truth.

This was due in part to the relatability of the script, but undoubtedly also due to the way Lisa Valentine Clark portrayed the main character. Lisa is a TV and movie actor with a long commercial résumé. She is also a mother of five, with all the home-life chaos that implies. And the ad is a hilarious mishmash of the highlights—or lowlights—of a mother's life, packed into just under four manic minutes. That authenticity connected.

You can see this in the comments on the ad. Dozens of fans left messages of "This is so me" or "This is my life" or "I totally get this mom." The script, and Lisa, genuinely captured what real life feels like to the target audience.

Ironically, Lisa wasn't actually the first casting choice. The competition was fierce, with over fifty applicants. And initially the client called for a younger lead. But her experience in comedy gave her quick comedic timing. Plus certain team members kept pushing for Lisa to be cast for the role.

And Lisa was already a fan of Chatbooks herself.

Lisa: "I've been a Chatbooks user for a long time. In fact—funny story—after the whole day of filming the ad, I came home and there was a brand-new Chatbook waiting for me. Kismet. It's a beautiful thing."

That connection of actors who are real-life fans is a consistent part of Harmon Brothers' success and Creative Process. Lisa was a Chatbooks user. Purple's Goldilocks (Mallory Everton) had actually slept on a Purple and loved it. The Camp Chef Grill God (that story coming up, don't get impatient) is not actually a god, but *is* an actual southern barbeque connoisseur. The twenty-first century is in love with "authenticity," but requires that the reality of the character be appealing to people. Jerks can be authentic all they want, and people still won't buy from them.

But if you love the product for real, then that will show in the writing of the script, the acting, and the video editing in indefinable, but powerful, ways. So be an authentic fan of what you sell.

Authentic fan, but with no system for channeling the enthusiasm, equals pushing hot air around without cooling anything. Clearly there's a process here—what is it?

Miracles happen when you sell something you believe in.
Make your own miracles by checking out the free content at
harmonbrothersbook.com/bonus

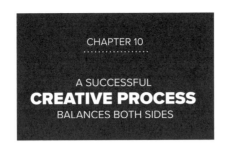

Modern workers like a culture where they feel empowered to do their best work without a lot of interference. We saw that in the Creative Culture section. Creative types tend to value these things even more than the average, and they congregate around a loose company culture.

Well, it's very easy to create a loose culture at a company: don't do any work.

That right there will take care of it.

If you never attempt to produce anything—don't place any load on the bridge, so to speak—you'll rarely have people at each other's throats, rarely get cliques or feuds, and almost never have any serious contention. A leaky pipe can look exactly the same as a sound one—until you put water in it. It's only when the system is charged, when water flows and pressure builds, that you can see where the cracks are.

Those cracks can be serious. In small companies they can—and routinely do—lead to the death of the company, at least in its original form. Pressure and stress are killers, both of people and of businesses. Yet they often cannot be seen until the crisis arrives, when it can be too late to repair the damage.

Which makes it all the more remarkable that Harmon Brothers has been able to maintain one of the loosest cultures in modern business, almost wholly reliant on adults making solid decisions that advance the work of the company, while churning out a very high volume of award-winning work for such a small group. There's a video of the Poo~Pourri CEO saying, somewhat dazedly, "I had no idea the rate at which this team moved."

Clearly the solution to incorporating an intentional Creative Process takes more than a loosey-goosey culture all by itself. Ad-hoc culture has a tendency to make the work produced either nonexistent or of poor quality.

To reduce that danger, the Harmon Brothers have designed a workflow that allows maximal creative freedom to the group, while still ensuring that deadlines are met and quality work produced.

First, the point person, a member of the HB Business Development team, scores a product in eight categories:

1. Does the team love it?
2. Is there an obvious problem that this product solves?
3. Does the product differentiate itself significantly?
4. Are its customers enthusiastic fans about the product?
5. Is the product ready for market?
6. Is it scalable?
7. Are the people at the company reliable and do they communicate well?
8. Do they trust us with creative control?

It can take anywhere from several weeks to several months for Harmon Brothers to work though this research phase.

Once a company and product scores high enough in these eight categories (discussed in much more detail in the Creative Partnerships section below), the company moves from research to proposal mode.

Benton Crane (this has traditionally been his gig) and a couple members of the creative team will present a formal proposal to the potential client.

Harmon Brothers charges "by the awesome." This means companies are committing at little more than half a million dollars based purely on what the Harmon Brothers have done before, and their representations of what they will be able to do for the client. Incidentally, unlike the industry standard, the actual content of the eventual ad is not a part of those negotiations.

Once the contract is signed, a writing team is assembled. This team is led by top humor/creative writers in the business, Dave Vance, Mallory Everton, Whitney Call Meek, Jonny Vance, Matt Meese, Natalie Madsen, Robert Mack, Brett Crockett, Lisa Valentine Clark, Jessica Rigby, Kellen Erskine, Alex Velluto, among others, for a full team of three to five writers.

The writers will spend a month to six weeks researching the company itself and then working through ideas. Harmon Brothers will spend tens of thousands of dollars on research and development in this phase to make sure the potential scripts will truly encapsulate the client's unique selling proposition.

Then comes the Writers' Retreat. These retreats take place at a secluded lodge among the aspens of the Wasatch Mountains. Those invited include the writing team, decision-makers of the client, Harmon Brothers team members, and documentary support staff. Sometimes a fellow writing a book about the company is lucky enough to go too. The retreat is two days of inspiring meals, wide-ranging conversations, and, ultimately, a shoot-ready script.

Prior to the retreat, each writer on the team independently develops an entire commercial of two to five minutes, something much like a comedy sketch. Harmon Brothers are capable of selling things with an eye to seriousness, but that's not the default. Heck, at least one writer says at nearly every meeting, "We have to have a poop joke. It's tradition." (This tradition has since been broken, but this book is bringing it back.)

Writers need to be able to check their egos at the door—inevitably, some of their favorite work will end up on the cutting room floor. That's just how editing works. For the good of the script, terrific stuff often has to be removed. For example, this book was originally 7,017 pages.

They read out their scripts to the assemblage, and then the clients and the creatives hash out which one is the best. That script becomes the template for moving forward on the commercial.

Only when the script is ready do they get to what most people think of as "moviemaking:" directing, camerawork, key grips, best boys and gaffers, etc. In other words, a lot of the work to make the movie occurs well before the movie is being "made" at all—before a single frame of video is shot. And a good deal of what makes a movie successful comes after all the moviemaking is complete—distributing the film to the markets where it will be successful, coordinating release dates, etc.

So it is with Harmon Brothers. Not until now does anyone even get out a camera. Everything up to this point is research and discussion and hard, hard writing to get the message precisely crafted. Then the usual suspects are put to work: soundstages, makeup, scenery, props, catering, and of course, casting and directing.

This last phase does, undeniably, involve a substantially greater number of people than either of the other two phases combined. It begins with a finished script—substantially finished, anyway—and moves from there to the standard process for shooting an ad.

Although Daniel Harmon is the chief creative officer, he still directs video (although he rarely gets the chair you see on all the movie sets). But any one of these several people could be the creative director on a given project.

Beyond that, there is a patchwork quilt of people hired, depending on what the script needs. Even those roles are often switched and moved about, depending on commitments to other projects and the inclination of different people to handle a variety of assignments.

Casting is a key part of the magic. The creative director is usually primarily responsible for casting the lead, and often that process can take a couple of weeks and even a couple of false starts (wait until you read about the BedJet shoot).

Knowing not only who can pull off the lines on a cold read but who will be able to handle the grind—and it *is* a grind with endless takes late into the evening—is more art than science. And then there's that indefinable something that brings the script alive. If you want to see examples, check out what Wes Tolman as the prince in the Squatty Potty ads or Lisa Valentine Clark in the Chatbooks ads bring to their characters.

Some of the shoots are exceptionally complicated, whether with motorized equipment—the cranes and cars of FiberFix—or animatronics—the unicorn and dragon from Squatty Potty. Some are more simple on the mechanical side but require more actors, like Chatbooks.

Harmon Brothers tries to get most of the shots done in a three-day run, but sometimes there is bleed (or extra shots) that require specialized skills, as in the glamour food shots in the Camp Chef hero ad (story coming soon).

With the footage in the can (film term for "finished shooting," and also the canning term for "putting something in a can"), they move along to the editing process, and here is where the bulk of the team is put to work.

A huge amount of work goes into chiseling terabytes of 4K or 8K video into two to five minutes of clean perfection. Sound is added, both music and effects.

Subtitling has to be completed—videos are watched much more often when people can read them as the video plays. This is because of the huge number of people watching them when they aren't supposed to be on Facebook in the first place.

The ads are edited, cropped, cut, polished, and readied for distribution. And I just used one sentence to describe what often takes weeks of long days and multiple all-nighters to get the job done right.

Then the moment of truth: the video goes live.

And the magic happens.

Nah. It isn't magic at all. Harmon Brothers has an entire team of people whose function, based on complex formulae, is to push the video into the places it will perform best.

Lots of companies make ads. Many of them make very good ones. In this niche however, it is rare to realize an immediate positive return on investment. Often ads are run more or less entirely for "exposure," where the goal is not an immediate sale but the expansion of the brand into public consciousness. Like a lion looking at a bowl of salad, Harmon Brothers is unsatisfied with such puny expectations.

A Harmon Brothers hero ad video is engineered to bring an immediate return on investment—and not just break even, either. With most clients, Harmon Brothers sets the bar higher than a dollar-for-dollar return.

As many as twenty people are part of this postproduction team, considerably more than in the other phases. But simply engaging large numbers of people doesn't automatically inflate the importance of that particular phase. Indeed, Harmon Brothers considers each phase to be equally important with the others, and they put their money where their mouths are, as we saw from the even three-way split of the profit allocation in the explanation on compensation.

This Creative Process is effective because it balances creative freedom with productivity. All well and good, when you have something like a Squatty Potty that doesn't have any competition but stopped-up bowels. What if you have to pit this creative process against a saturated market?

Hold on to your hats, 'cause here we go.

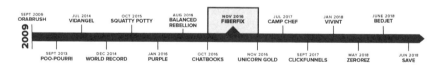

SEPT 2009
ORABRUSH

2009

SEPT 2013
POO-POURRI

JUL 2014
VIDANGEL

DEC 2014
WORLD RECORD

OCT 2015
SQUATTY POTTY

JAN 2016
PURPLE

AUG 2016
BALANCED
REBELLION

OCT 2016
CHATBOOKS

NOV 2016
FIBERFIX

NOV 2016
UNICORN GOLD

JUL 2017
CAMP CHEF

SEPT 2017
CLICKFUNNELS

JAN 2018
VIVINT

MAY 2018
ZEROREZ

JUNE 2018
BEDJET

JUN 2018
SAVE

FROM POOP TO GOLD

CHAPTER 11
....

FIBERFIX

{ *In which Harmon Brothers'*
creative process rolls another ad
down the mountain. }

I t's 2016, and the summer sun bakes the FiberFix shoot
location, with the crew retreating to the hot shade of tents,
desperately glugging water. The set is next to a gravel pit cliff,
with two Geo Metros prepped to "drive" off the edge. The cars
are encased in protective metal cages—the cages held together
not by welds, but one with common duct tape and the other
wrapped in the innovative FiberFix. Which tape, if any, would
hold together around a car tossed off the side of a cliff? (Is this
question a cliffhanger? Why yes, yes it is.)

FiberFix is the brand name of a fiberglass tape that competes in
some applications with one of the world's most used products:
duct tape. Duct tape was originally known as Duck Tape and
was invented by a mother to protect her son's rifle rounds from
getting wet in the beach landing at D-Day, another thing I did
not make up.

No matter how you spell it, most American households have a
couple rolls. The crew of Apollo 13 used duct tape—or perhaps
Duck Tape—to fix their spacecraft and provide another link
in Six Degrees of Kevin Bacon. It's an American icon. In fact,
competing with such an established brand could get . . . sticky.
Yes, that's a Benton Crane joke.

FiberFix challenged an industry already saturated with players. They were even told there was no point in continuing to develop their idea. But Spencer Quinn, a founder of FiberFix, knew their product was distinctive and decided that if Harmon Brothers could advertise poop sprays and mattresses, they could probably pivot and do something compelling for a fiberglass tape too.

Harmon Brothers took a look. They normally aren't interested in saturated markets, but they were already fans of the product, having used FiberFix (donated by the FiberFix company) on a video for VidAngel in 2014.

They agreed that FiberFix was different than duct/Duck Tape. It fulfills a different role in the tape niche—instead of sticking as a single strand, it wraps—like casting a broken arm—and forms a rigid fiberglass material that is "as strong as steel." Making a FiberFix hero ad got the green light.

Key for FiberFix was a kind of advertising they could dial up and down at need. FiberFix isn't a large company, and product inventory and supply was an ongoing problem. Selling more product is terrific if you can meet the demand, and success, while wonderful, creates problems that have to be solved. Every year or so, FiberFix was having to move to bigger warehouses, necessitating two weeks of downtime. They had appeared on *Shark Tank* in October of 2014, and though they received a huge spike in orders, it wasn't controllable or forecastable (as most ad response is not).

Most *Shark Tank* applications are binned, as they say across the pond, but once in a lightning strike the product is intriguing enough to get a call and a chance on the show. FiberFix had that kind of mojo. Funny story, the call from the *Shark Tank*'s producers was the first FiberFix had heard of their application. Someone else sent it in for them and didn't bother to tell them. They went on and scored a deal (with the same Shark that later invested in Squatty Potty, oddly enough).

"We got a huge spike in orders, and then we declined and plateaued," Spencer said, using his arm to show the wave. "The plateau was higher than it had been before, but it wasn't where we wanted to be. We wanted something farther up the curve," he said, pantomiming a rising slope. "The burst was great, but it just isn't something you can staff up for. It's almost like it created more problems than it solved. We wanted something we could turn on and off, that we had more fine control over." Something, in fact, like a Harmon Brothers hero ad.

By now, Harmon Brothers had honed its Creative Process and they rolled out the full Harmon Brothers treatment, starting with in-depth research, script writing, and a Writers' Retreat in Sundance, now a Harmon Brothers' tradition.

What came out of it was a redneck repairman's dream. The commercial features Jason Gray, from comedy troupe Studio C, using FiberFix to repair everything from broken fiberglass tent poles to a rake to plumbing. But the centerpiece of the hero ad was the tagline, "Strong as Steel," and Harmon Brothers needed a way to demonstrate that.

Jason Gray
FiberFix Spokesperson

The first idea was to build a ramp out of steel piping, with joints secured by FiberFix, then drive a three-ton pickup onto the ramp. Benton had been a high-school champion mechanic and was only too happy to work on the machinery for that.

But although the FiberFix was up to the challenge, the video didn't really pop. The demonstration wasn't effective enough. They needed something flashier, something with more visual wow.

How about building a roll cage out of steel and FiberFix, wrapping a car up in it, then driving it off a cliff? Yeah. That will work.

And it did.

Benton, Theron Harmon, and James Dayton, HB Assistant Director on this project, spent weeks looking around Utah for a place to crash a car. In the end, a series of coincidences led Benton and the Roundys, a father-son special effects duo, to an abandoned  gravel pit right on the edge of Utah Lake. It faced west, so the light would be good, and the cliff was suitably steep with a long, flat run-up which even Geo Metros could drive.

That's Metros, plural, because for an effective demonstration, you need two cars—one to go over the cliff in a cage secured by a dozen rolls of duct tape, and the other to go over in a cage of FiberFix. Actually, you need six cars. Two for testing in preproduction and four film-ready cars, because two of those are backups for if something goes sideways.

The FiberFix held up well in the trials, but, you know, this was a *car.* Nobody knew for sure if it would work.

Theron: "We had tested it all we could. We were pretty sure it would hold up, but we had a lot riding on the outcome, so no one was certain."

Except Spencer. "I knew it would hold. We'd done all the testing on it, and we knew that it literally was as strong as steel. It would hold up just fine. My only worry was that the shot wouldn't be good, that the car wouldn't roll well, or the light would be gone, or something like that."

The rest of the shots completed, the crew set about rigging for the most ambitious stunt in Harmon Brothers' history.

Then came the wind.

It howled in off the lake in vicious gusts, blowing about camera equipment and kicking up dust. On a movie or commercial set, time is literally money, as everyone there is billing by the hour. Having to pack up and come back the next day would risk a change of lighting from the first day's shoot—always tricky—and weather, and cost tens of thousands. So they waited, drinking gallons of water in the blistering heat. When the wind slacked off, there was only time for one shot per car.

Cameras placed. Sound rolling. Here came the first car.

It vaulted off the cliff at twenty miles an hour, hung in space a moment, and plummeted. It slammed into the hillside in a cloud of sand and rock. The duct tape held for part of one car roll, and then began shredding like smoked pork. Chunks of metal pelted the cliffside. The crash dummy exited the vehicle through the driver's side window. More or less a perfect demonstration of what not to do.

But would the second take show the difference? Would FiberFix really be strong enough?

Second car on the way. Sun slanting low over the lake, about to be swallowed by the Oquirrh Mountains to the west. Cameras rolling. The red car trundled down the dirt road and onto the ramp just short of the cliff edge. Out into space, spinning. Falling. Smashing. Rolling.

Resisting. Holding.

FROM POOP TO GOLD

The car got pretty battered. But the cage held, just as Spencer knew it would.

It rolled twelve, fourteen times, down the hill and away along the flat stony ground, like a Chevy Tumbleweed. Rocking over once more, it came to rest on all four tires. A pause, as the dust floated. Then the cheering began.

The video, released in August 2016, experienced some technical headwinds (more details in the ClickFunnels story coming soon) but eventually positioned the brand right where FiberFix wanted.

Theron: "We drove FiberFix online sales to an initial burst of 20 times more than they were before. And over the course of the next year, they saw increases in retail that they could only attribute to the campaign. For instance, when they'd go to conventions they would booth next to big companies in the adhesive space, like 3M. But they found that retail purchasing agents considered them along with the mega companies (even though they were a hundredth the size of the biggest players)—the buyers knew the FiberFix brand, were impressed by it, and wanted to partner."

As of the fall 2018, the video had been viewed over thirty-five million times. Clearly a strong Creative Process *can* overcome the difficulties of a saturated market.

Time to uncover the secret ingredients of the Harmon Brothers' Creative Process.

*No message can be clearer than pushing a car off a cliff. Clarify your message by watching the free videos at **harmonbrothersbook.com/bonus***

FROM POOP TO GOLD

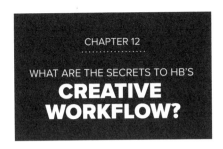

M ost creatives have a process they follow; although, there's a myth that Mozart didn't need one.

The world at large tends to have the impression that Mozart sat alone at the piano, sipping a light chardonnay, waiting for the inspiration thunderbolt to strike and the 17th Symphony to come rolling out.

There's a reason for this, and it has to do with a clever, but somewhat pointless, fraud. In 1815, a German publication called the *General Music Journal* published a letter from Mozart to his father, in which he said this:

. . . Provided I am not disturbed, my subject enlarges itself . . . [and] stands almost finished and complete in my mind . . . I hear them, as it were, all at once. When I proceed to write down my ideas, the committing to paper is done quickly enough . . . it rarely differs on paper from what it was in my imagination.

In other words, Mozart says his creativity is easy and painless.

Too bad the letter is a lie.

No one is quite sure why the fraud was perpetrated, but it's been a successful one. Although the letter was first debunked as early as 1856, it has been quoted thousands of times over 200 years, including this morning in a meme on your Facebook feed. Seriously. Go check.

Harmless, though, right? No. Destructive, actually. Because Mozart did not work that way. In fact, the opposite is true.

His manuscripts are filled with revisions, scribbles, annotations, and excisions. In other (real) letters, he often described the difficulties he labored under and the agony of the process of getting the melodies and harmonies to work together. I mean, he didn't write his first symphony until he was eight.

Right, well, he's a genius. But still, he had a process, and it wasn't divine. It was both imagination and refining, creative and productive.

And that's the whole point of Harmon Brothers' Creative Process—balancing the creative and the productive; the artist with the editor.

There are four ways Harmon Brothers maintains this balance:

1. Deadlines

"We are dead serious about deadlines," says Benton Crane, who is not in charge of humor at Harmon Brothers. But he isn't kidding, either. "We've only missed one deadline. Ever. And it was a big deal, even though it was a small deadline. But it's never going to happen again."

Deadlines are one of the secrets to keeping the balance between creative freedom and work.

Daniel: "We set a date of delivery, and then schedule backwards and so these mini deadlines become set. And everyone knows exactly what needs to happen and when."

Benton: "When I'm out selling a client, we'll talk about a launch date and some clients will be hesitant to pull the trigger on something, worried that we might miss a deadline. But I know our staff. And I can promise that we will meet the target date."

The reverse, though, is also true. If a client wants a deadline Benton knows the team can't meet, Harmon Brothers will turn down the contract. Deadlines protect the client, but they also protect the team. Both sides must win, or there's no deal.

2. Good Ideas Come from Anyone, Anywhere, Anytime

From Anyone:

No matter the title or weight of responsibility, everyone at Harmon Brothers is encouraged to offer opinions, solutions, and ideas. It doesn't matter if the debate is between Daniel and an intern, the weight of Daniel's position as Chief Creative Officer doesn't determine the quality or validity of the idea.

Jonah Rindlisbacher started out as an intern sweeping floors at Harmon Brothers. Within three years, he became an HB producer and video editor, as well as pivotal on the Save the Storks video.

Jonah: "As editor while working on Save the Storks, we found ourselves struggling with how to present the story. A second

Jonah Rindlisbacher
Line Producer

recording of the interview came out stale. Daniel made me feel that he believed I was somehow better equipped to find a solution to the story than he was. You better believe I worked my butt off to find an answer.

One exhausting night after a week of intense editing, I was trying a new edit structure, and I ran into some footage of the narrator beginning to cry—footage that I'd overlooked previously because it didn't share any information or push the story forward. But I had tried so many other things at that point that in near desperation I threw it in the edit. Suddenly, the barrage of information disappeared and there was a step change in story. Rather than simply gathering the events of the main lead's story, I found her emotion. Suddenly the little holes in the narrative didn't really matter. I perfected the edit and showed it to Daniel."

The more emotional edit touched them both to the point of tearing up.

Daniel: "We knew the video struck an emotional chord that would resonate with others, and the entire story needed to build to that moment."

Jonah: "That edit did not change very much and is very close to the current state of the now finished video. I was just the editor but Daniel gave me the final word on that story. It not only made the story work, but it also changed how I thought about my own work and made a profound mark on my life."

Good ideas can come from anyone.

From Anywhere:

Tyler Stevens, an HB postproduction supervisor: "We noticed that as consumers shifted to viewing video on their mobile phones, it made sense to shift our ads from a horizontal 16:9 to a vertical 3:4 aspect ratio. But it is challenging to tell a story vertically. And no one else was doing this."

But good ideas can come from anywhere, and this one came from Batman. Really.

Even though no one notices when they watch his movies, Director Christopher Nolan uses something called variable aspect ratios. His movies *Dark Knight, Dark Knight Rises, Inception,* and *Interstellar* all change in size on the screen. Sometimes it'll be a long cinematic rectangle, or it shrinks in from the sides, making it more square. It's a tool to focus viewer eyes on where he wants them.

Harmon Brothers' creative types paid attention to that. They adopted Nolan's variable aspect ratio idea and applied it to mobile advertising, testing to see if they could make it work..

Daniel: "We use the portrait style when we're doing a close up on someone's face. But when we pull out the shot, we squeeze it down from the top and bottom, making it rectangular or landscape, and add text or graphics on the top and bottom of the wide shot to fill the space. Sometimes we stack information above and below to better communicate our message. This changing aspect ratio is becoming more and more common. But to our knowledge, we are the ones who pioneered its application to mobile video."

And now it's industry standard.

At Anytime:

Nothing is set in stone at Harmon Brothers. Even if it's twenty-four hours before the shoot or forty-eight hours before launch. The drive for quality means no idea can cure into concrete until it's uploaded and published.

Daniel: "We don't lock in scripts or cuts of a video. Everything is flexible, until it isn't."

Understandably, this drives subcontractors crazy, as it makes the project a moving target. But they prep their subcontractors with the advice to build a cushion into their bid, of both time and money. Because Harmon Brothers will keep pushing to improve, even if it's inconvenient.

While in the last video editing stage of the Zerorez hero ad (the Zerorez story coming soon), when the video was close to finished, a pivot in the direction of the ad had Shane Rickard, an HB creative director, up all night workshopping a completely different cut of the video. Shane and Nick Ritter, HB finishing editor, both put in eighteen hours that night and morning to make the new cut a reality.

Nick: "I do think the new version was much better, which made it easier to put in the extra time. This reworking process happened a few times throughout Zerorez's postproduction."

And that is why Harmon Brothers takes ideas anytime—because it makes the project better.

3. Creative Control

Harmon Brothers expects creative control over each advertising project, and thoroughly prequalifies clients.

Daniel: "Clients choose us, out of everyone else in the world, to do something that they can't do themselves—so let us do it. Let us do what we do best."

One potential client had a great product that passed the passion test, which means after using it, the Harmon Brothers team felt passionate about the usefulness and quality of the product. But the founder of the company had been on *Shark Tank* and had been the face of his previous ads (he self-describes as a "media whore"), and he wanted to be the star of the ad. Harmon Brothers was not convinced that he was best for the ad, so they parted ways.

Another instance had one client threatened to be kicked off a Harmon Brothers set because she was interjecting too much.

James Dayton
Creative Director

James Dayton: "It is integral to Harmon Brothers' magic that we own the entire process from strategy to concept and script, to preproduction, production, and postproduction, to distribution, and finally to optimization and PR support."

During the Squatty Potty shoot, Squatty Potty's management team didn't even show up to set since they had a simultaneous industry conference and made that a priority instead.

Chatbooks only showed up on the set for four hours out of a three-day shoot, explaining that they didn't want to mess with the magic.

FiberFix showed up to watch the car fly off the cliff—of course—and see actor Jason Gray give some lines. But that was it.

ClickFunnels joined Harmon Brothers on set for a couple hours on one day, and otherwise trusted that the system would do the work.

But it does go both ways.

Daniel: "Ultimately, we have to trust the client, that they can deliver on driving a campaign, scaling product, and keep up on customer service."

Creative control is all about trust—and it's trust from both sides.

4. Have a Brain Trust

Committees get a bad name. They also get bad *names*, like the Joint Select Committee on the Solvency of Multiemployer Pension Plans—a name I did not make up.

While it is true that committees can be a way to stop a group from taking action (a great example is from a film I decline to name, where a planet gets invaded and instead of doing something about it, the Senate organizes a committee to look into it), it is also true that a small group can often make *better* progress than a large mob of people in an entire company. A committee can more efficiently divide up tasks and implement specific action with a minimum of fuss, as long as the committee doesn't become an HOA.

Harmon Brothers has a committee known as the Brain Trust. There's one on each project, with each member chosen by the creative director. The HB Brain Trust only meets when needed, and only has one goal: to point out problems.

For instance, the Brain Trust will meet to review the final script, point out any jokes that fall flat or don't fit the client, and note where the flow of the ad needs reworking. The Brain Trust's perspective allows them to connect the Harmon Brothers' WHY of Share Better Stories to the needs of the client and selling the product.

The mantra is one you'll hear from a lot of people at Harmon Brothers: Sales first, art second.

Again, the Brain Trust's function is not to solve problems, but to identify them (or predict where they will emerge). They poke holes and make suggestions for improvement, but it's up to the project team to find the solutions.

The Brain Trust's advice looms big in Harmon Brothers' lore with the Purple Mattress Egg Test.

The idea of the Egg Test, dropping eggs attached to a sheet of glass onto a mattress below, was a Brain Trust idea (Jeffrey, again). But initially the demo was buried, not appearing until more than halfway through the video. When the Brain Trust saw the nearly completed ad, they immediately identified the Egg Test as the most compelling part of the video.

Benton: "They said, 'Hey guys, this Egg Test *is* the video. You need to get it right up front.' So we did. We had to redo the entire order of the ad, but that was what we needed to make it work best."

Purple is now one of Harmon Brothers' most successful ads, with almost half a billion views.

5. Prioritize Quality over Profit

Harmon Brothers has a budget to produce a video. Of course they do. But if they don't feel the video performs to a high enough standard, then they'll reshoot and reedit to make it the way it needs to be. Does this break the budget? Initially, yes (so don't try this at home with your personal finances).

Daniel: "But we're thinking long term. We feel that this will build a better brand long term and create a more long-lasting relationship with the client. As the ad performs better, we'll get more clients too. All parties are served better by us living by this principle. And *we* are more proud of what we create."

What if the ad isn't successful *enough*?

Daniel: "One ad was producing a dollar out for every dollar in. That made the ad worth it to the client, but it wasn't enough for us. We wanted a stronger return for our client and felt that our video could do better."

So Harmon Brothers put in their own money to reshoot the video. And . . . so far, it's converting better (see the Zerorez story coming up).

Daniel: "Prioritizing quality over profit can be an expensive principle to live by, but we know that it makes an ad more successful, and more business comes to us because of that success. And in the end, that makes more money for everybody."

To review, these five points are:

1. Deadlines
2. Good Ideas Come from Anyone, Anywhere, and at Anytime
3. Creative Control
4. Brain Trust
5. Prioritizing Quality over Profit.

These are some of the secrets to how Harmon Brothers' Creative Process protects and encourages creativity, ensuring that quality work is accomplished.

As internally, between the company and the employees, so it is externally, between Harmon Brothers and clients. If it's going to be a partnership, it has to work for both parties. And not just kinda work. It has to thrill. Like Disneyland. Like Niagara. Like an escalator and a four-year-old.

That kind of partnership doesn't come by accident. It takes disciplined work to find out, long before the cameras roll, that both companies are going to get great things from working together. How does Harmon Brothers do that work? Glad you asked.

PART 3

CREATIVE
PARTNERSHIPS

{ *How do you determine if a product and company is excellent enough to disrupt markets?* }

CHAPTER 13

CURATING
PRODUCTS & CLIENTS

In 2017, Harmon Brothers received over 1,200 unsolicited leads, inquiries from companies that were considering working with Harmon Brothers as an ad agency.

That's far too many for a company whose top volume for a year stands at around ten campaigns. Weeding through those thousand plus leads takes huge HB resources, and on the other side, no one likes to be told no.

This is one reason Harmon Brothers pushed aside the curtain so I could write this book. Because the pattern they have for curating products can help any company measure their product's excellence, whether they end up partnering with Harmon Brothers or not.

Benton Crane
CEO

Benton: "People come to us all the time with a mediocre product hoping that we will be their silver bullet. It doesn't work that way. We believe world-class marketing married to world-

Working with Harmon Brothers— well before a finished ad is even on deadline—can have serious benefits. One company, seeking financing, asked for permission to tell investors that they were "in discussion" with Harmon Brothers to have the ad agency do their product launch. The investors, not fooled by the circuitous verbiage, responded that they would be happy to invest, once the discussions had produced a commitment.

class products is the best recipe for disrupting markets and creating household brand names."

As mentioned previously, Harmon Brothers has a seven-step filter process to determine if a product (and the company behind it) is a good match:

1. Does the team love the product?

The team has to love the product themselves, or they won't take it on. Many companies, eager to have Harmon Brothers become familiar with their product, send unsolicited cases of it to HB Headquarters (hence the fridge full of craft versions of Rockstar). Few days go by without the UPS guy delivering anything from cups that can't be knocked over to planners to canned sandwiches (yes, canned sandwiches . . . *finally*).

Before they'll seriously consider working with someone, Harmon Brothers will have several members of the team try it out and give their opinion on the product.

If there are agents of the US Treasury reading this, Harmon Brothers wanted me to say that they would like the opportunity to test some samples of your product—preferably nonsequential, used, and in blocks of a thousand. Thanks in advance.

2. Is there a real problem that this product solves?

If there isn't, then to be successful the product would have to be sold to people who don't need it. That's not a Harmon Brothers thing, for a number of reasons, the simplest one being that it's really hard to sell things to people who have to be talked into wanting them.

Being politically liberty-minded and frugal (you should see the rusty 1989 Hyundai Excel that Neal Harmon drives), they are highly reluctant to do any psychological strong-arming. If the product doesn't make a case for itself, it won't make it to the contract stage.

3. Is it a "Blue Ocean" product, or at least a product that differentiates itself significantly?

Is the product discernibly different from any other product on the market, with no product similar enough to be significant competition? Does it have a lot of market space and very few competitors? Products on the margin, or in "red ocean" space, where the competition is fierce and the differentiation is small, generally compete on price and do not have the growth path that Harmon Brothers is looking for. Although, Harmon Brothers has been known to take on "red ocean" products (like mattresses and tape for instance) if the product is unique enough.

4. Is it loved by its customers?

What are the Amazon reviews saying?

Blue oceans have been around for millions of years (or somewhat less, for those of you in the public schools of Tennessee), but blue ocean, the business concept, is only a teenager. It's a concept from *Blue Ocean Strategy* by W. Chan Kim and Renee Mauborgne. It describes the process of creating and backing only products that have nothing but blue ocean around them, where there is no effective competition, where they have uncontested markets. The concept of trying to invent a product that has "no competition" is centuries old, of course, and as elusive as the transmutation of lead to gold; what is new is the ability to connect to the niche markets where the competition is at least at best muted. Facebook, Google, and others that specialize in data dicing can serve up targeted markets and give products more advantages than ever before.

Seriously, this was a huge reason the team took a contract with BedJet and Camp Chef. Consumer reviews are very important and get a mention in nearly every video that Harmon Brothers produces.

The product has to satisfy. Delight, even. It has to be worthy of the energy it will take to market it effectively. By the way, and this isn't a big deal, but I personally like five-star Amazon ratings as well. Just by way of information. Thought you'd like to know, you know, as a kind of quirky fact about me. Anyways, yeah . . .

5. Have they nailed the product?

It has to be wonderful, and work precisely as advertised. If a company is still tinkering with the product, if it still needs iterating to make it exceptional, then it's not ready for the structural stress of a Harmon Brothers launch.

Harmon Brothers helped Purple with their branding, product, and packaging before it was ready to launch. This is unusual, and Harmon Brothers prefers for the company to have already prepared this on their own.

This does not require that the product be perfect, only that it be considered finished with proven market traction. An idea, even a great idea, is not enough.

6. Is it scalable? Is there a sufficient market size for this company to dominate the niche?

The Poo~Pourri and Purple ads were so hot they blew the doors off manufacturing, leading to delays, unhappy people, and negative buzz. A viral ad is like holding on to the fin of a rocket as it accelerates through the atmosphere—your hair burns off if your space suit isn't ready.

Harmon Brothers wants to help companies *dominate* their niche. It doesn't always happen, but that is the ideal. Accomplishing this goal requires a company to have the infrastructure, know-how, manpower, and supply chain built to fill the demand.

To transform from making a solid living to becoming a true industry giant turns out to be a very difficult transition for a company to make. This may sound odd—after all, who wouldn't want to develop their small firm into a huge company that dominates its market? But it's not possible to get there without risking something, something warm and comforting.

Most companies, to make the transition, have to take a lot of the profit margin and plow it back into growth. That's scary. And most companies won't do it. Harmon Brothers looks to work with companies willing to take the risk to make the transition.

7. Does the company act professionally?

Life is too short to work with jerks. To mention anyone by name would make me one, so even though I *absolutely* could, I won't. Because I'm not a jerk. Like some people.

Instead, I'm just going to list these four signs that a company is potentially toxic:

A. *They stop responding to you, but expect you to read their mind.*

B. *They ignore your boundaries.*

C. *They take credit for all success rather than reflecting it to their team (an early indicator is how someone describes past successes—do they describe it with "I" or "we"?)*

D. *When stress is full bore (whether from success or failure), they blame and get angry.*

Come to think of it, that's a pretty good set of indicators in *any* relationship. And no, I didn't get these questions from a Buzzfeed relationship quiz.

8. Do they trust us with creative control?

I mentioned creative control earlier, and it's part of Harmon Brothers' client filter as well as their culture. It's integral to their creative process.

One reason Harmon Brothers feels so strongly about holding onto creative control, is, as Benton explains, "all our biggest successes have come from clients that have trusted us to do our thing. They've given us their car keys and opened up the road."

Daniel Harmon
Chief Creative Director

Daniel: "It's about trust. If they aren't going to trust us to do our work, then we won't work with them. We're not a factory for hire. We are more than just a video production company."

This is the criteria for getting a date with Harmon Brothers (although, HB has made exceptions if a product is particularly innovative).

More importantly, a product and company that meets all eight of these requirements has a chance to disrupt a market and be a household name—as in these behind-the-scenes stories from four successful Harmon Brothers ads.

SEPT 2009 ORABRUSH	JUL 2014 VIDANGEL	OCT 2015 SQUATTY POTTY	AUG 2016 BALANCED REBELLION	NOV 2016 FIBERFIX	JUL 2017 CAMP CHEF	JAN 2018 VIVINT	JUNE 2018 BEDJET

SEPT 2013 POO-POURRI	DEC 2014 WORLD RECORD	JAN 2016 PURPLE	OCT 2016 CHATBOOKS	NOV 2016 UNICORN GOLD	SEPT 2017 CLICKFUNNELS	MAY 2018 ZEROREZ	JUN 2018 SAVE

CHAPTER 14

CAMP CHEF

{ *In which a unique smoker snatches market share with a grill god's help.* }

I t's early spring in 2017, and I am in the middle of nowhere—Kamas, Utah—on the set of the Camp Chef hero ad.

"Can you do that again, only this time a little bit less with the left hand? Don't wave it about so much." says Daniel Harmon, who is directing this shoot. He stares intently at the monitor where the god's image is displayed.

Daniel Harmon
Chief Creative Director

"Surely," responds actor JW Hutson in a genteel Southern accent. The Grill God is dressed in a white toga, with a leafy gold crown, a golden tool belt, and natty sandals.

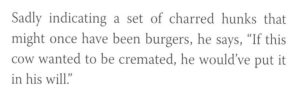

Sadly indicating a set of charred hunks that might once have been burgers, he says, "If this cow wanted to be cremated, he would've put it in his will."

J.W. Hutson
Grill God

His voice rolls out like the aroma of smoking ribs. Which, as it happens, this particular grill can also create. It's an innovative meshing of the backyard grill and a supremely simple smoker, by a company just breaking into the high-end grill market.

The company is called Camp Chef and, among other things, it has developed the Woodwind, a beautiful, versatile, and easy-to-use piece of equipment that does the precision job of an expensive, labor-intensive hardwood smoker, except without the labor. "A little bit of wood, a little bit of wind" the Grill God himself will pronounce here in a minute.

But the initial partnership between Harmon Brothers and Camp Chef wasn't easy. It almost didn't happen.

Traeger is the (sometimes disputed) leader in the smoker grill space and contacted Harmon Brothers about doing work with them. Jeffrey Harmon had a Traeger in his backyard. He loved it. A number of the boxes on the "Do we work with these guys?" list were checked by Traeger, and there was, through the summer of 2016, a fair amount of chatter about whether the Harmon Brothers would take on Traeger as a client. It seemed a natural fit.

But then Camp Chef contacted Harmon Brothers in August 2016 and made a compelling pitch.

Travis Simon, then Camp Chef's director of marketing: "We wanted them to know that we had something truly special, something that set us apart in the marketplace. We have patents pending. Also, we sponsor a cooking show on the Sportsman Channel, so we know something about the media side of things. Our grill truly is unique. We knew they [Harmon Brothers] were probably talking to other people, but we really, really wanted them."

What convinced Jeffrey was the Amazon ratings coupled with the versatility of the grill itself.

"Traeger has good ratings, which you'd expect, but Camp Chef's were off the scale. I thought they'd be a better fit for us." Being able to grill and smoke—plus sear the finished product—on a single machine, was the clincher.

Working on this project was a bit different than moving low-price items like poop spray and tongue brushes, as the Woodwind smoker grill retails around $800. That price point compares with Purple mattresses, which Harmon Brothers knows something about as well, but unlike a mattress, most people don't think they *need* a smoker grill. They're wrong, but not everyone has tasted Woodwind brisket, so it's forgivable.

Daniel: "We knew we wouldn't have the impulse buys on this one like we did with FiberFix, but we thought the product lent itself to our, um, irreverent approach."

As HB branched off their initial scatological successes, the range of products they represented grew as well. This was their first culinary one. Though perhaps the theme is still there: pooping (Squatty Potty)—everyone poops; sleeping (Purple)—everyone sleeps; and breaking things (FiberFix)—everyone breaks things. Harmon Brothers intentionally goes for products that scale, that are potentially the kinds of things millions of people will want, and this is in that same line. Everyone eats, don't they? Well, why not eat really, really well?

At the Camp Chef Writers' Retreat, the HB team, Camp Chef team, and writers gathered for the second reading of the script. During the pitch session earlier, the three competing scripts were each so funny that by the end Theron Harmon was wiping away tears (I pick on him for convenience—he had a lot of company). But in the end, the vote was for Jonny Vance's script.

Jonny was a writer for Studio C, as opposed to an on-screen actor, and his quirky sense of humor turned out to be just the ticket. His pitch revolved around a man trying to become the heroic barbecue master of the cul-de-sac. The man gets help from the God of the Grill, a Greek-style god in a toga—but with a southern drawl—that intervenes to make his dreams come true, along the way extolling the virtues of the Woodwind as the perfect tool for the job.

Jonny Vance
Lead Writer

Daniel led this part of the discussion. He began with a disclaimer. "This is still far from a polished script. We're going to refine it from here."

Jonny got up to read the roughed-in script, southern accent floating out there, mellow and smooth (though a far cry from what JW would later produce on camera). And the laughs began.

The reading proved that the script was, truly, very funny. Not as hilarious as it would eventually be, but it was funny, and it built as it went along, with the biggest laughs toward the end.

The Camp Chef representatives liked the read. They laughed in all the right places. But they weren't sold yet, and their comments were pointed and realistic.

Travis: "The line 'You like great food, but you don't have the time or the talent to be a great chef' doesn't resonate with me. I'm a guy, and I think I have the talent to do pretty much anything."

"We went for the alliteration there," writer and actor Matt Meese said. "Time and talent."

"What about 'skill'?" Daniel said. Words flew. Suggestions from everywhere. The line was changed, and changed again. Four times. Five. The writers chiseled away on the script in real time as things were suggested (thanks, Google Docs). Editing the initial blocks of stone, trying to reveal the true form of the thing inside.

"What about changing the whole line," Matt said. "You like five-star food but don't have the time to be a five-star chef?"

It read well. It "landed," as the comics say. But if you've seen the video, you know that the final version put the alliteration back in, only in a different order: "You don't have the *tools* or the *time* to be a five-star chef." Yes, this is what professional word-craft looks like. Except it's even more boring, sometimes.

In a four-page script every line, every word on every line, matters. Stand-up comedy is relentlessly unforgiving in this way, and sketch comedy is closely related. There is a huge difference between a funny line and a dead one, in terms of audience reaction. But being able to tell that difference in the written script, or in the practice run, is a skill few mortals possess. Which word is funnier, *snicker* or *giggle*? It depends on a thousand things. These people are professionals precisely because they can, more often than the rest of us, tell which word to use.

After finishing an editing session just among the writers, Daniel took the floor: "And now, there's one thing more I want to ask about, and that's the creative process here. I don't want to break something that's working, but if there's a way to do this that doesn't fit the way we've done this in the past, I want to hear it."

He was, in true Harmon Brothers fashion, analyzing, testing, and asking about the whole system, "Is this effective or just traditional?" As mentioned earlier in this book, though there is a defined system in place, it has to be examined to see if it meets the needs of each client. There is no hesitation in confronting what isn't working, no matter how well it has worked in the past. The team is pleased. The process is rolling smoothly.

Theron poked his head in. "Dinner is in thirty minutes," he said. "How close are you?"

Daniel: "We can finish up in fifteen minutes, then do another read-through before we eat."

A new joke, saying that five Cuban cigars is not how smoking meat works, rocked the house, and the "Grill God forgives you" joke got solid laughs. But there's more to this hero ad than humor, and the Camp Chef people insisted that this come through in the ad.

Brandon Sparrow, COO of Camp Chef: "We have to pitch this as the do-all grill because nothing else works as well as this one to cook every kind of food you can imagine. It's got a sear box, it's got wood pellets, it's got everything."

The nods all came from the Camp Chef side of the room. They know grilling. Travis launched into an explanation of why sear boxes work, discussing protein breakdown and flavor profiles. It's a unique product, their grill. The Camp Chef people were critically interested in making sure the ad explained the grill's unique features, and not so concerned with overwhelming a potential customer with information about how the unit works.

In the end, Harmon Brothers essentially had to say, "Look, this is why you're hiring us. We know how to reach the audience you want to target and get them to buy your grills." The Camp Chef team believed in the expertise of Harmon Brothers. At the end of the retreat, the roughed-in script remained largely intact.

The key figure in the script was the Grill God, and he needed to be southern and preferably a bit long in the tooth. A man with seasoning. JW has a thicker southern accent, more rural, and when he speeds up, he sounds a great deal like Morgan Freeman. A *great* deal. In the end, JW won the audition, and a few days later shooting began.

Shooting the Camp Chef hero ad took place in a warehouse-looking building that isn't a warehouse at all, but a massive complex that's been the soundstage of ABC's *Blood and Oil*, among other shows. It's a cavernous space, broken into four soundstages, of which Harmon Brothers occupied about half of one. Their backyard barbecue set had faux grass carpeting the floor—complete with realistic-looking plastic shrubs—around a flagstone patio.

"And I said, let there be *smoke.*" The Grill God stood there under the lights, with his array of golden tools on his barbecue belt, ready to make you a believer.

The operation for Camp Chef ran a few thousand an hour for rentals, personnel, and space. Movie work costs incredible sums. Delays burn cash, but even doing the work on schedule spends it the way flooding rivers carry off levees.

Remember, none of this generates a thin dime of revenue for at least another six weeks. The first rough cut had to be completed in less than seven days, by the timeline.

Why that fast? Well, the time frames are terrifically compressed on every Harmon Brothers shoot, but this time there was another dimension as well.

The ad depended heavily on close-up glamour shots of food.

Theron Harmon
Client Happiness

Theron Harmon: "The food is the product. What we're selling isn't the grill, it's the *food*. The taste of the food is the critical element. If people connect with that, we did our job."

But none of the Harmon Brothers team were sufficiently experienced with filming food. It's practically an art form all by itself.

Theron: "In the end, we thought it would be silly not to cover our bases comprehensively and get the best talent we could for such an important part of the video."

Harmon Brothers obtained the services of the world-renowned Simon Paul, a London-based food cinematographer. Yes. That's a thing.

As you might imagine, getting this guy wasn't cheap. Theron, who is notoriously, um, tight with a buck, ran budget management on this shoot. He kind of pursed his mouth when asked about this, the look of a guy that got something sour in his last mouthful of pie. "We did talk a lot about it. It's going to inflate our budget quite a bit to have this guy come in, but Shane and Daniel felt like we shouldn't skimp on this part of the project."

After a bit of discussion, Theron relented. "Look, it seems like a lot of money up front, but think of it this way. Suppose it makes a difference in the response rates? Won't that be worth it, over several million views? That's how I'm looking at it. If getting the world's best food director of photography means a 5 percent better conversion rate, we will have spent that money well. There's a reason they pay this guy tens of thousands per shoot and fly him all over the world."

And the risk paid off. After testing various video openers, the winning intro was Simon's food shots. BBQ ribs splitting apart. A perfect steak landing on the grill. A slo-mo shot of a hamburger patty smoking. Viewers connected to the food. And the return on investment was repaid several times over.

But that was yet to come. Harmon Brothers still had the video launch. And they wanted to try something a little different for this hero.

Tiffani Barth (she'd been with Harmon Brothers less than a month at this point) worked the last details for a huge Camp Chef launch party. The grand opening would bring in hundreds of people to sample actual food from the grill.

Tiffani Barth
Project Manager

I asked her about it a week before launch. "We hope for about 400 people. So far we have . . . " she squinted at the screen, "223. So we have a ways to go."

This launch was scheduled during a workday—a Wednesday, to avoid the buzzkill of Thursday. Apparently, Thursday is a terrible day to release a video. That statement will just have to stand there like a lone pine in a meadow because although there are reasons why, and the team has tried to explain them, they don't make enough sense that they can be passed along. So, Thursday is bad—it's like the Monday of the middle of the week. Keep that in mind, if you ever try this yourself.

The launch was timed for the early afternoon. The hope was that the afternoon would give the ad time to boost that day, with hundreds of people tweeting it, Instagramming it, and Facebooking it (imagine saying that sentence to somebody in 1998). This abundant chatter was designed to help it hit the appropriate algorithm, making it onto the Now Trending right-hand bar on Facebook (and other promoted lists on social media channels).

As the launch drew closer, Tiffani began to look . . . not stressed, exactly, but definitely up to her neck in work. Was it because of the impending deadline, or because putting a huge party together is harder than producing a commercial?

Tiffani: "It's actually not all that dissimilar. Producing is something I know about, I've done it before, but event planning *isn't* something I've done. I've had to do a lot of research on it to make sure I'm doing all that needs to be on the list. Printing, signs, decorations, the venue, all sorts of things. I even called the fire department to make sure that when we have six smokers filling up their sky with wood smoke that they won't be showing up to close everything down." And then she invited the entire Provo FD to the launch too, because nothing makes friends like smoked meats.

T-minus one day. The site of the launch party was quiet, the calm before the storm. The video editors still blasted away on the final edits of the ad. The punch list—those things that still remain to be done, like eliminating some glare from a quarter-inch of cheese—was very long and the video editing team got no sleep the night before.

At Harmon HQ, though, there was no dashing frantically about. Although the usual semi-random chaos was nowhere to be seen, replaced by laser focus. The presence of the deadline had a wonderfully sharpening effect. Every screen—four, five of them—had a cut of the ad. Each pair of eyes scanned for something out of place.

"Comma right there," Daniel said, pointing. He and Jonah Rindlisbacher reviewed the subtitles. Videos with subtitles do much, much better than others, because of the number of people that are watching them in environments where noise is not welcome. These days, most people *read* their videos. This was the first Harmon Brothers ad to have subtitles fully baked into the video on screen (this means the subtitles cannot be turned off so HB controls exactly how they display and integrate with the whole piece).

Tiffani clicked to a new screen. Attendance. She worked down the list. The scrolling this week took a lot longer than this time last week. "415 now. We're picking up a lot more today. It's not the 500 I was after, but it will work. They won't all show, of course. But maybe we'll get some walk-ins."

If I recall correctly, last week she was hoping for *four* hundred guests. When you hit your target, move it back and shoot again.

A voice floated out of the other room. "Whoa. We have a new winner. This new intro is much better." That's Abe Niederhauser, then HB lead media buyer (and now cryptocurrency god), whose job was to push the video out to people. He tested five different versions of the commercial—the first thirty seconds only—and crunched the data to find out which one people stuck with longest.

Abe Niederhauser
Lead Media Buyer

The version that opens directly on the Grill God saying, "Bad grillin's a sin! REPENT!" had been leading the pack. But then Abe tested a different one, one that starts with ribs, fillet mignon, steak, hamburger, all glory shots of meat in slo-mo (thanks to Simon from London). Imagine the movie *300* but with steaks instead of Spartans.

His pronouncement about the new test leader drew a gathering.

"That's a significant difference," Theron said. The ad, creatively named #5, had a 25.2 percent view-through rate of its introduction. The other contender was #3, with 23.6 percent.

That didn't look like much of a difference to me.

Abe: "The difference isn't 2 percent, it's 10 percent. Video #5 is 10 percent more effective. Think of that percentage for twenty million views over six months. That tiny difference is over 400,000 potential customers. That's a beautiful number." Abe smiled, like a father over his precocious child.

Pixels moved. Sounds were inserted. The file was buffed and polished right in front of me, and probably would be for the next twenty-two hours. Not that I was going to stick around for all of it. Writing is brutal. I needed my rest.

The next morning, it was the day of the launch. Savory Woodwind smoke wafted over central Provo. And oh, did it ever smell divine (Grill God approved this pun). Five chefs, all working away on their Woodwind grills, displayed their creations for the throng, which grew minute by minute although there were still about forty minutes before the official event began.

"I think we're ready," Tiffani said, no note of panic or even stress in her voice. "We topped out at around 530 tickets issued, which is like a hundred in the last two days. So I'm optimistic. We're as ready as we can be."

By the far wall, just off stage left, Abe had his laptop open, scrolling through feeds. Ad #5 did indeed hang on to the lead long enough to be tabbed the winner. It will become the official version of the ad in about an hour and a half.

"Ready?"

Abe smiled. None of these people ever seemed rattled. "You bet. Except the live feed is not . . . wait, let me refresh. There it comes."

The event was broadcasting live on the Camp Chef page on Facebook and had just come up on their page. Traffic jumped to a couple hundred viewers in a matter of seconds.

A bird's-eye view on the proceedings showed a space that would be comfortable for 200–300 people. If they got 500 people trying to get in, Tiffani might regret having invited the fire marshall.

Brandon Sparrow, Camp Chef COO, wandered up, with a small smile on his face. He's pleased with how it's all come together. "Love it. Really great venue. Everything looks great. The final cut of the video is terrific. I think it's going to go really well."

When asked what he would say was a home run on the launch, he thought for a second. "Anything. Really. I want the crowd to be jazzed, and to get good food and a solid intro to the product. You know, liking the video and stuff."

Really? No sales number, or anything?

"Nah. There's a long lead time on this thing. We know that. We're just excited to launch in a new way. I'm not even going to look at sales figures for like a month."

Then in staggered Jonah. Literally. Staggered.

Was the video done?

"As done as human frailty can make it," he said. His bloodshot eyes had huge bags hanging underneath them. His wife Sarah stalked over and propped him up with a smile and a kiss.

"Good morning," she said. "Nice to see you."

He smiled wearily. "We didn't go home last night," he said to me by way of explanation. "We were working on subtitles and loading everything up until about five minutes ago. I think I'll sleep for a couple days after this."

A buzz went through the hall as the MC took the stage, and the video screen dropped behind him. "Okay, friends, the time you've all been waiting for is here. Who's ready for the world premiere of this video?"

Video #5 rolled. Meat sizzled. The grilling master wannabe woke from his dream, licked his lips expectantly, opened his grill, and groaned. Nothing there but burnt patties. And then:

"Bad grillin's a sin! REPENT!" thundered the Grill God.

Away they went.

Simultaneous to this, the ad went live all over the internet, YouTube, Facebook, Instagram, everywhere. Abe bent over his machine, reading the immediate response off the laptop screen, refreshing like the dipping pump of an oil derrick. His face radiated calm.

JW, the Grill God himself, appeared to general applause. He waved to the assemblage. He looked the part, toga and golden toolbelt firmly in place, and his smile, like everything else he does, was thoroughly genuine.

Abe refreshed. "Share rate is good. But then, we'd expect that from the crowd here. So far so good, I'd say."

The whole Camp Chef team was invited to assemble on stage for a photograph. There was much hugging and backslapping, along with a row of very, very tired video editors sitting on the front of the stage. It was the end of a long season. Except, really, it wasn't.

There is understandable temptation to see video launches as the final game of the season, with well-earned time off coming on its heels. But for the HB team, all they've done is throw the opening pitch. The ball is still in the air, with the batter stepping into his swing. It is only once the video is in the wild that their game can begin to produce, and we can find out if the team is good enough to win. They're the ones who are tasked with making the hard work pay off.

And pay off it did.

By the end of the first month, the video hit 4.8 million views. Sales increased from a few per day, to 25–30 per day within the first month of the ad's run. Even better, the rate of return on ad spend turned out substantially stronger than Harmon Brothers had predicted in discussions with the client.

Benton Crane got a minute to talk about this a couple weeks after the ad went live. "We're seeing something between four and five dollars of revenue to one dollar of ad spend in our return metrics. We thought three to one would be excellent; all our projections were based on that kind of response, but we're doing a lot better than that so far."

In other words, for every dollar Camp Chef spent on ad promotion, they saw four to five dollars in revenue. It's a perpetual money machine. And the ad continued with its strong numbers.

RELATIVE ONLINE SALES

CAMP CHEF

Data by SECOND MEASURE

60X

40X

20X

OCT '12

GRILL GOD
MAY '17

Just over a year later, Harmon Brothers' Camp Chef ad campaign has been viewed over 20 million times, with a couple of sidekicks and a reimagined hero ad (launched May 2018). Camp Chef has not yet overtaken Traeger as the leader in the pellet grill space, but Camp Chef has disrupted the market since the launch of the video.

Perhaps, down the road, Camp Chef will become the king of the mountain in pellet grills. They have the team and the product that can do it. For now, the Creative Partnership is an indisputable success and their future is bright. "Hot ham!"

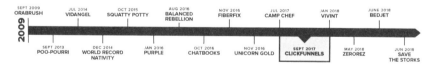

SEPT 2009
ORABRUSH

JUL 2014
VIDANGEL

OCT 2015
SQUATTY POTTY

AUG 2016
BALANCED
REBELLION

NOV 2016
FIBERFIX

JUL 2017
CAMP CHEF

JAN 2018
VIVINT

JUNE 2018
BEDJET

2009

SEPT 2013
POO-POURRI

DEC 2014
WORLD RECORD
NATIVITY

JAN 2016
PURPLE

OCT 2016
CHATBOOKS

NOV 2016
UNICORN GOLD

SEPT 2017
CLICKFUNNELS

MAY 2018
ZEROREZ

JUN 2018
SAVE
THE STORKS

CHAPTER 15
....

CLICK FUNNELS

{ *In which a disruptive pitchman and a reconsidered partnership go digging for gold.* }

It's late summer 2017, on the set of the ClickFunnels ad. A massive stylized gold mine, carved and painted from styrofoam, lines the back of the warehouse wall, looming like a Disneyland ride, complete with a mining cart on wheels. Actor Christopher Robin Miller is kitted out like a prospector, saying, "So if you like making money, and don't want to murder your dreams, go to ClickFunnels.com."

ClickFunnels is a true twenty-first-century venture, a company whose claim to fame is its ability to take a web funnel's visitors and, through a series of questions and calls to action, sift the right visitors into paying customers. It's a rags to riches story, built on sweat and no outside investment.

Benton Crane first learned about ClickFunnels back in 2014 while preparing for a shoot that required almost a thousand volunteers, a massive number to coordinate. Derral Eves, associate producer on the project, volunteered to create a website to coordinate everything.

Benton Crane
CEO

Derral Eves
Consultant

A few short hours later, Benton got the link to the website in an email. Benton, no stranger to how long these things generally take, was shocked at how fast Derral was able to put together such a slick website. "It was the kind of thing that would have taken me days," Benton said. It was a ClickFunnels template. Benton looked up ClickFunnels, liked what he saw, and filed that info away.

Fast forward to 2017. Harmon Brothers completed and launched an ad for FiberFix which quickly reached 18 million views. Then, without warning or explanation, it vanished. For reasons still not understood (and Harmon Brothers was not the only one to experience a disappearing video during this time), Facebook removed the FiberFix ad off its platform (a month later—again without explanation—the video returned to Facebook, but the early buzz was gone).

As soon as the ad vanished, Harmon Brothers scrambled all hands. They were able to relaunch the ad (although, sadly, without the millions of views already collected). It scored likes and shares, and plenty of thumbs up on YouTube, but sales struggled to regain momentum. Maybe, the team thought, it's not the ad that's the problem.

So they went through the buying process, as if they were a customer. Going through the FiberFix website, Harmon Brothers found that it took five to six clicks for a buyer to checkout. It was an obstacle to closing sales. That's when Benton remembered ClickFunnels.

Not knowing that ClickFunnels CEO Russell Brunson had become a celebrity in his own right, Benton called him up directly. Sometimes the shortest way is the best way. The ensuing

Russell Brunson
ClickFunnels CEO

conversation, ironically, revealed that while Benton wanted Russell's expertise to streamline the ordering process for FiberFix, Russell himself had been following Harmon Brothers and wanted to do a deal for his own company.

Benton: "Russell asked us, 'If I fix your checkout problem, will you make me a script?' We agreed—if he could double our conversion rate. It took some work, but he did it."

Daniel Harmon was skeptical that the two companies would be a good fit. ClickFunnels is, in all the important ways, Russell Brunson, and Russell's in-your-face style wasn't a natural extension of the Harmon Brothers vibe. After all, Russell talks about the cult of ClickFunnels and wears a t-shirt that says, "CULT-ure."

Benton: "We didn't have plans to have a full campaign for Russell. We were going to deliver a great script in exchange for the help he'd given us on the FiberFix deal and move on."

So they scheduled the script read-through. Things began to change at the Writers' Retreat.

Daniel: "We found that we liked Russell. His public persona is a little bit intense salesman, but at the writing retreat, we realized he is a genuinely awesome human being who wants to make the world a better place. We were more aligned in our ideals than we originally thought. Although he still runs around like a gerbil on speed all the time."

The Harmon Brothers team returned from the writing retreat enthused about the project. They had had a great experience working with the client, and they were so happy with the script that they shared it around the office.

Tiffani Barth: "Everyone loved the script and agreed that it had the HB magic. We felt a little bummed that we weren't going to make it into one of our videos."

Tiffani Barth
Project Manager

Luckily that changed fast.

Benton: "As the writers—particularly Jonny Vance—researched the ins and outs of ClickFunnels, they fell in love with the concept as well as the script. It's a really good product."

A key difference between ClickFunnels and other online systems is that ClickFunnels focuses their funnel templates on turning visitors into customers, whereas Squarespace and Wix just focus on providing pretty templates.

Gradually, the team was convinced. Everyone bought into the idea of doing an entire campaign for ClickFunnels.

Theron Harmon: "We were able to bring a new style of marketing to ClickFunnels. Their ads were rapid fire, super low budget, and they pumped them out daily. They wanted to try something that brought a new flavor and a new voice to their brand. And that something was us."

Theron Harmon
Client Happiness

Initially Daniel Harmon was going to direct this ad. But the shoot dates interfered with a campout with his son that he felt was too important to miss. So he offered the director's chair to Kaitlin Snow Seamons, who had been a critical part of

Kaitlin Snow
Lead Editor

the success of several hero videos without ever bringing her yellow beanie to the big chair.

Harmon Brothers gives you opportunities to grow when you've proven yourself in the past. If you do a good job in one area, you'll get chances to prove yourself in others.

For Kaitlin, one of the things that differed from video editing to directing was being able to choose locations for different parts of the script. The scripts come with the speaking parts and main characters, but minimal stage direction and settings. When you're the director, you get to make the decisions.

Kaitlin: "With ClickFunnels I knew I wanted a cavern. I could just picture that gold digger in a cave. Daniel's only worry was that it'd be too dark. But I told him it'd be straight out of Snow White, a place people would want to be. And doesn't everyone want a cave full of treasure?" She got her cavern.

The scene with the sparkling cave in the background was shot in a production-designer warehouse—which was good, because there was no way that set was transportable. The design team reused styrofoam of a devil cave from a previous shoot and carved out the mine, with a tunnel in the center, a minecart, and rails.

One reason the set was so large was because ClickFunnels was the first hero ad Harmon Brothers shot for a 3:4 aspect ratio. Up until then, the aspect ratio was cut down during editing, which proved to be very difficult because the framing of the action had to be particular. Sometimes bodies would be cut off in the smaller aspect ratio. But the 3:4 format is the cutting edge format for in-line Facebook videos. It's more vertical. And it means that for filming, the background needed to be both wider and taller than the typical 16:9 aspect ratio they were used to.

Kaitlin: "When they were building the set, I walked in to check it out. They were doing an awesome job, but it was too small. I had them add four feet to the top so we could get the shot wide enough."

However, the video needed to be able to launch on YouTube as well, which still used a 16:9 aspect ratio. In order for editors to prepare videos in both formats, most shots are simply filmed from farther away, so the action takes place in the center of the screen. Then editors can crop the video to different sizes from the same shots.

Kaitlin: "To make sure the action would fit in the 3:4 space, we got in the habit of using guides on the director's screen monitor. I'm glad we were thinking about the different filming formats when we were filming the office scenes because we had to place the camera farther out so it was wide enough for the 3:4 format but the characters could be close together without it feeling awkward. Sometimes we'd do a shot twice, one for 3:4 and one 16:9. But not often. Usually we'd just shoot so it could be used for both."

Nick Ritter
Finishing Editor

This new 3:4 format had a learning curve with graphics too. Nick Ritter was over graphics, and this was his proving project for Harmon Brothers. As is typical for newbies, he was offered a particular role on a specific project to see how he did. And he did fabulous work, especially when patience was called for. Initially he built the graphics in 3:4. They looked great. But when he reformatted the ad for 16:9, the graphics were stretched. Nick redid them all—every single one—for the additional format. In the process, he figured out that going from 16:9 to 3:4 works just fine, so in the future the process would be a lot easier.

The graphics turned out to be a vital piece of the ClickFunnels hero ad.

Kaitlin: "ClickFunnels was an extra challenging campaign because there wasn't a physical product to hold up and say, "Buy this." We had to make sure

Most of the creative team at Harmon Brothers began as interns. Kaitlin worked at Orabrush and edited a new video every Tuesday. Tyler and Shane started at Orabrush too, proving themselves with low pay and long hours. At Harmon Brothers, if newbies work hard on their proving project and fit the team and culture, then their team members fight for them to be hired. "I secretly hope that it will click for people, that they'll see this is a great company to be creative in and a place where you can do what you love to do," adds Kaitlin.

we could communicate what a funnel was, and that was very graphic intensive. We had to thoroughly understand how the platform worked so we could explain it easily ourselves."

In the script, the gold digger character paints nudes—nude squirrels, that is.

Kaitlin decided to show how the gold digger would easily create a funnel for selling his artwork. But showing how easy something is can get very complicated.

Kaitlin: "I had a list of twenty different shot instructions of where the mouse needed to click and what we needed to see the pages doing. I was very specific in what we needed."

And the format issue reared its head again. A computer page is set at a 16:9 aspect ratio, so when the graphic was a computer screen, the displayed website had to be changed to fit the 3:4 aspect ratio, doubling the work.

Kaitlin: "I'd never directed graphics before. It's a whole different process. Nick and I worked out a system where he'd audition the graphic almost like an actor. After Brett Crockett made the characters, Nick animated them. At first he'd rough in only the key frames and explain what the animation would do. If we liked them or after we made any changes, then he'd animate the in-between shots too."

Not all the problems were graphical—Kaitlin's choice of locations put the shoot up the river. Literally.

In one of the ad's early shots, actor Christopher, in full miner regalia, is sitting on the side of a river as if he were panning for gold. An actual river. Pretty. But not inclined to alter course just so it could get into a commercial.

Tiffani: "That was a rough day. To get to the river, it took a ten-minute walk carrying equipment through a marsh. Christopher didn't have to cross the river, but the crew did, and then for an important closeup shot, they had to wade into the water while holding the boom pole steady for sound. The river was running fast, pretty dangerous, and there was no embankment to set a camera on. The location was stunningly beautiful but difficult for a camera crew."

Finally all the shots were edited and graphics animated. It was time to see if the messaging worked—had they explained ClickFunnels in a way that a viewer would catch on immediately?

There's only one way to know. You have to test it.

Members of the creative team headed to a nearby university with dozens of donuts and a couple iPads to show the ClickFunnels ad. They asked passing students, "Can I trade you five minutes of your time for a donut?" After showing the video several dozen donuts' worth, they knew what needed to be changed.

Kaitlin: "The biggest problem was people thought the Steve character was a seller of something like the gold digger. They didn't get that he was a customer learning about ClickFunnels just like the viewer. So we had a reshoot to fix some things. We try not to reshoot, but if we have to do it, we do because we aren't going to release shoddy work."

The video successfully launched. Because there wasn't a physical product to be sold—the ad encourages entrepreneurs to become ClickFunnels subscribers—Harmon Brothers set their target for the cost of acquiring a customer, and by the end of the first two weeks, the ad was beating that target.

Theron: "It's a hilarious ad, and I'm glad we decided to make it because it helped ClickFunnels' business. But Harmon Brothers would not be what it is right now without Russell. Because of his advice, we created Harmon Brothers University to share what we've learned about making ads that sell well. That is straight out of Russell's playbook."

Christopher Robin Miller
Gold Digger

Actor Christopher as the Gold Digger: "ClickFunnels. If it were any better at taking people's money, it'd be called the IRS."

The Creative Partnership may not have been love at first sight. But it doesn't always have to be.

The FiberFix Facebook disaster led to a ClickFunnels hero ad, a better ClickFunnels, and a better Harmon Brothers. Sounds like a gold mine to me.

FROM POOP TO GOLD

CHAPTER 16

BEDJET

{ *In which a meticulously designed product solves a devilish problem to heavenly reviews.* }

It's late spring 2018, and I am on the set of the BedJet commercial watching the light check and actors receive their makeup. Actor Natalie Madsen walks in and says, "Hi, Gavin," to the man in the muscular red demon suit sitting in the makeup chair.

But it's not Gavin. It's actor Noah Kershisnik who stepped into the part a mere forty-eight hours earlier. That was when actor—and HB operations manager—Gavin Bentley discovered he was claustrophobic as he hyperventilated inside the tight-fitting foam suit. So the last forty-eight hours have been a panicked scramble to find a replacement actor. Does it count as a miracle if you find a perfect demon?

Mark Aramli, CEO and founder of BedJet, had approached Harmon Brothers saying, "I have looked around; I want to work with the best, and your company is the best." He has a deep smooth voice that sounds custom built for radio work.

Mark Aramli
BedJet CEO

Jonny Vance
Lead Writer

Initially, Jonny Vance, creative director on this project, was excited when BedJet reached out to

Harmon Brothers. He thought the product was great. Small problem—he was actually excited about a *competitor's* product.

Jonny: "I said, 'Mark, I heard so much about this, Tim Ferriss even talked about it.' Mark responded, 'No, that's the wrong one. But it's okay because ours is better. Go look up that product's reviews, compare them to mine, and then make your decision.' And I did. And BedJet's reviews were amazing."

As a former NASA engineer, Mark is a meticulous man who prides himself on his customer care as much as his product. He once spent twenty minutes showing Theron Harmon BedJet's enthusiastic customer reviews on Amazon.

"This right here is the payoff as an entrepreneur," Mark said, pointing out a particular Amazon review that shows how BedJet helped a woman sleep in spite of the hot flashes of menopause. For him the reward was about improving lives as much as financial wins. And he personally responds to almost every Amazon review.

Theron Harmon
Client Happiness

Theron Harmon: "His consistently high Amazon reviews is one of the reasons we decided to check out his product. What blew us away was that BedJet had the highest rated reviews of all the 30,000 mattress products on Amazon."

But originally Theron was skeptical of the BedJet. He didn't really see how a unit that blows air through a comforter would be something people would be interested in buying. Frankly, it sounded like a gimmick. But Mark had science on his side and a truly intellectual approach to the problem his product was solving. Against his first impression, Theron found himself intrigued.

Then Mark sent over four BedJet units for them to try.

Theron: "Mark didn't want to send a whole bunch of units. He wanted to just send over two, but we got him up to four so that the writers as well as team leaders could try it out. When we got them, both Jonny and I fell in love with the product. It was clearly unlike anything we'd ever experienced. Our wives loved it too, and we all use it to this day."

By this point, Harmon Brothers was interested enough to take a closer look at BedJet. With four different potential clients on the east coast, Jonny and Theron planned a trip to visit them and on that trip spent an evening and a day with Mark and his BedJet team.

Jonny was impressed by the vibe from the plain offices in the historic district of Newport, Rhode Island. BedJet had humble digs just like Harmon Brothers. And like Harmon Brothers, what happened inside Bedjet's offices mattered more than their exterior.

Entirely satisfied with the trip, Harmon Brothers moved forward with a Writers' Retreat. Interestingly, two writers independently presented the concept of a demon character married to a human woman—something that hadn't happened since two writers brought Goldilocks to the Purple mattress retreat. Mark took this as a sign. He liked the idea and was willing to take the risk of such a script.

Once the scripts were merged with the best of all three, then Mark's engineer personality came out.

Jonny: "The retreat was very . . . thorough. We read the script sentence by sentence, as a NASA scientist would. Of course,

Mark *is* a NASA scientist, so." From the grueling process came one of Harmon Brothers' funniest scripts. But finding the right demon actor was no simple task.

Casting normally takes two to four weeks. But casting for the demon character took almost double that. Hundreds of actors auditioned. The first choice was vetoed by Mark. He asked Gavin to do a read. And everything clicked. Then it was on to the custom-created costume.

Jonny: "We knew we needed to make this demon costume, and coincidentally we were able to work with Chris Hanson, who not only made the unicorn for Squatty Potty, but he actually worked on the demon suit for the movie *Hellboy*. That we were able to get him to make our demon suit was pretty awesome."

The costume was molded to fit Gavin's body, then the mold was cast in an oven (no actors were harmed in the making of the costume), then made into a silicon foam suit. With muscles sculpted into it, large tattoos, and two ivory-colored horns, the suit was exactly what Harmon Brothers envisioned. Finally finished, Gavin came in for the fitting two days before the shoot.

It took two hours to squeeze Gavin into the costume. Then Gavin started having a panic attack. There is being uncomfortable in tight spaces, and there is claustrophobia, and then there is being sealed into a foam rubber body-and-head suit. No matter how hard he tried, he couldn't stop himself from panicking.

Gavin Bentley
Operations Manager

Jonny: "We had to find an actor that could take it—after taking six weeks to find the last one. We had forty-eight hours. AND he had to fit into a suit cast for a lean body. It was tense."

The assistant director volunteered a friend named Noah Kershisnik that he knew from his improv class. Noah not only had the comedic chops, but he was accustomed to spending long days in tight latex body suits (don't ask). So they gave him a call.

Noah walked in to try on the suit and Chris Hansen took one look at him and said, "Sorry, you're not going to fit." Noah was both taller and bigger than Gavin. But they decided to try anyway. They used a plastic grocery bag to squeeze the costume over Noah's head. It took three of them to wrangle him into it.

Jonny: "We begged the suit to fit, and it did, and then we're realizing, 'Wow, okay, this worked! Now we have to get Mark to sign off on him.' By this time it was early morning, and Mark was on his way to the airport to arrive for the shoot. We got him on the phone, and he trusted us enough to say, 'Let's do it.'"

Halfway through the grueling shoot, Noah developed a latex allergy, so he did the remaining days of shooting covered in rashes and hives. Two hours to get into the suit, four hours cooking under the BedJet and blankets, and another hour and a half to get back out of it. Good thing Noah channeled his inner demon because it was pretty close to hell.

Or maybe just Purgatory because the shoot eventually finished. And postproduction began. Which was *actual* hell, depending on who you talk to.

Daniel Harmon
Chief Creative Director

Daniel Harmon: "We had a extremely tight deadline, and there were some rough all-nighters. But after the ad was live, people were saying, 'Where did you find that demon guy? He is so good!'"

Although people seemed to love the ad, it didn't explode like Harmon Brothers' other viral ads. Facebook had (again) tinkered with their algorithms and it took a while to figure out how to put the ad where it would perform best. But once they did, it took off.

The share rates kept going up. Hundreds of commenters said they thought it was the best ad ever (although it should be noted that *every* HB ad gets that same response). Some suggested that it should be a sitcom.

Theron: "We'd never seen a share rate increase like that before. They usually stay flat or decrease after the initial few days."

And people were actually listening to the ad at full volume.

Benton Crane: "Facebook now recommends to bake in subtitles, but they didn't back when because we pioneered that trend. People typically want to watch with the sound off because, let's face it, they're at work and aren't supposed to be on Facebook."

Jonny: "For this ad, though, 75 percent of viewers actually turned on their sound. We credit that to people asking, 'What does this devil sound like?' It was phenomenal."

Jonny Vance
Lead Writer

In combination with very smart efforts by the client, BedJet sales are up over 200 percent over the prior year.

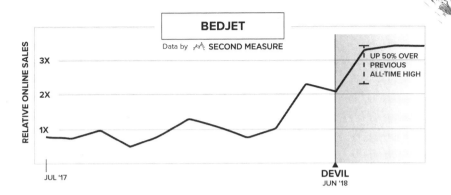

BEDJET

Data by SECOND MEASURE

RELATIVE ONLINE SALES

3X

2X

1X

JUL '17

I UP 50% OVER
I PREVIOUS
I ALL-TIME HIGH

DEVIL
JUN '18

Although a frugal businessman, Mark was so delighted with the success that he sent over ten more BedJets, so the whole Harmon Brothers team could have one.

The Creative Partnership worked because the BedJet is an outstanding product that could scale, and the devil was in the details.

FROM POOP TO GOLD

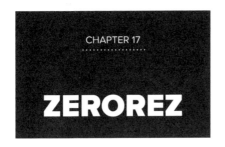

CHAPTER 17

ZEROREZ

{ *In which when the boots hit the ground,*
the best carpet cleaner rises to the surface,
refreshing the rest of the industry. }

I t's late summer 2018, and I am on the Zerorez set watching Harmon Brothers make a second hero ad for the carpet cleaning company. While the first ad launched earlier this year was themed as a Mexican soap opera, this ad is more scientific based. Actor Austin Craig (the spokesman on the first Orabrush commercial seven years ago) is back in a white lab coat using facts to compare Zerorez carpet cleaning to the competition, "In technical terms, those other guys leave behind a lot of crap."

Like some of Harmon Brothers' other clients, Zerorez competes in an industry that is mature and, most would say, saturated with competitors. There is no shortage of companies offering to clean your carpets—odds are there's a coupon in your mailbox right now.

Zerorez began in the '90s in Dallas and has since expanded across the country. As a franchise-based company, the carpet cleaner represented a unique challenge for Harmon Brothers' business model—the video could be authorized by the corporate office, but would the franchisees want it? And who was going to pay for it?

Chris Carson is the director of marketing at Zerorez. He's got to be older than he looks because he appears to be about fourteen. I forget about that immediately because he's so enthusiastic about his company and the partnership with Harmon Brothers. Turns out that enthusiasm is  a large part of the reason that Harmon Brothers made a carpet-cleaning video. In fairness, Harmon Brothers is a good deal of the reason Chris is at Zerorez too.

Chris: "I was at Chatbooks, just part of the marketing team there, but I got to see how the process worked, and of course I've been a huge fan of Harmon Brothers right from the beginning."

Chris' familiarity with Harmon Brothers was part of his interview at Zerorez.

 Shawn Moon, CEO of Zerorez: "I knew Chris was a Harmon Brothers fan, and that was an attractive thing for him to bring to our company. I hoped we'd be able to find a way to get our companies working together."

And they did.

But it took some massaging, and a fair amount of guts.

"It's kind of a funny story," Chris said, not laughing. "I brought up the idea of working with Harmon Brothers when I first came over to the company. The reaction was, um, not all that positive. I was actually told by someone that we would never, ever make a video with Harmon Brothers. It was just too much money to spend. I make a presentation every year to the franchisees at our annual conference. It's supposed to be about marketing budgets, initiatives, and company growth, and that stuff—and it was, but at the end I threw in a bunch of clips from Harmon Brothers videos and said I wanted to go for our own video in the next year."

The presentation didn't go over so well with the board.

In fact, Chris nearly got fired.

But he had planted the seed. The franchisees were not terribly excited about it, either, mostly because of the cost. Harmon Brothers charge "by the awesome," and that makes them expensive. But it's worth pointing out that charging by the awesome is a marketing strategy that can only work if you produce work that is, in fact, awesome. And Chris felt Harmon Brothers' work qualified, so he wasn't giving up.

Chris: "In the end, the only way the video was going to get made was for corporate to pay for the whole thing itself, which we did. All the franchisees had to do is pay for the distribution." He smiled. He risked his job over this thing, and he drew a straight flush.

Shawn joined us at HB Headquarters and popped his head out of the lunchroom, where he had obtained some crackers and cheese. He saw us and walked over, which gave me a chance to ask him what the response had been to the first video, launched about ten days before.

"Well," he said, clearly having answered this question before, "Dallas was one of our earliest adopters, and their results are coming in. Their online bookings from Zerorez.com were up 500% over the previous year. We take that as a good sign."

Five *hundred* percent?

Chris' smile widened. "*All* our franchisees are seeing increases, even the ones that haven't pushed the video in their areas. The virality of it is getting them increases in business without them spending a dime. The video is that good."

But under the surface things were complicated. The franchises are scattered around the nation, so they do their own ad buying. This meant that the standard Harmon Brothers model had to be extensively modified to work for Zerorez. Back at corporate, Benton Crane explained some of the details.

He pointed at his computer screen. "Here is an example of the problem. Since all the ad buy is being done franchisee by franchisee, we had to custom design a system that would handle orders coming in by zip code."

This particular screen showed a steeply ascending line, like the flight path of a Navy fighter off a carrier deck.

"This is the response rate, which is good. But here," Benton taps a key, and the line disappears, "we have another franchisee. So far, they haven't spent any money at all. We had to design a system that would track all fifty or so of their locations across thirty states."

Always before, there was a single point of contact at the corporate level, and the order for ad spend would come down from that point. Simple. But this? It's like Zerorez is fifty different companies. Because, actually, it is.

But Harmon Brothers solved that problem because that's how it was going to work best. Did it increase the budget? Yes. Yet the resulting system was robust enough to allow each franchisee to see their ad spend, order flow, and return on investment on a custom dashboard.

Benton: "They can decide, within a range, how much they're willing to spend to acquire a customer. It depends on how aggressive they want to be. But the franchisees that are putting the ad out there, yeah, they're getting a great return."

But was it going to be successful *enough*?

Daniel: "In the initial two months, this first Zerorez ad was producing at least two and half dollars out for every dollar in. But that wasn't enough for us. We wanted a stronger return for our client and felt that our video could do better."

Some of the Harmon Brothers team kept thinking about a key point of the original concept that didn't end up in the Mexican soap opera hero ad.

The benched idea circled around a machine that the team calls the Boot Test. Three carpet samples were dirtified, then each cleaned a different way: dry chem, steam, and Zerorez. Then the custom-built machine ran boots of various types over the three carpet remnants to simulate months of foot traffic. Voilà! When they checked the carpets for residue, only Zerorez carpets remained clean.

Harmon Brothers shot the Boot Test footage, and then . . . didn't use it. This might be difficult to imagine, but in a video simulating a Mexican soap opera, there wasn't a logical spot for it.

Hey, it happens. Harrison Ford was in Steven Spielberg's spectacular hit *E.T. the Extra-Terrestrial* all the way to the final cut. And then he wasn't. Seriously. Look it up.

However, unlike Harrison Ford's footage, there was a way to use that footage after all—IF they made another video, a second hero, a more technical and scientific-ish video. Understandably this took a great deal of discussion. One does not simply make another ad when the first one is successful and just launched, does one? Yes, apparently one does, if one works at Harmon

Brothers. The team felt that they could make a more compelling video, one that would out-success the first video.

Not only that, but after they put it together, they found the footage so compelling that they actually accelerated the launch of the second video to get it on the street sooner.

And they paid for it all themselves.

Yes, you read that right. Harmon Brothers thought they could do a video that would perform better than the original. So they put together a new one. Gratis.

And it worked. The more technical script and the boot testing machine really did make a better hero ad for Zerorez. It's newly released, but so far, it's converting better.

Earlier in the book you might remember the Creative Process secret Prioritize Quality over Profit. Harmon Brothers really does live this. Even though it broke their budget, they put quality first.

Back on the set, actor Kelly Vrooman is eating chocolate pudding and comparing it to how clean Zerorez leaves carpets, "It's all the good, without the bad. It's like eating pudding without the calories. That would be amazing."

And amazing is how the Creative Partnership worked between Zerorez and Harmon Brothers. Both companies agreed on the same principle: sometimes you have to take on more expense in the short term to get the quality long-term results you really want.

PART 4

APPLYING THESE
IDEAS TO
YOUR COMPANY

{ *Truth is, no business book is
more than a pleasant story if the
lessons remain on the page.* }

For the book to do what it's designed
to do, you need to find ways to bring
these principles to life and make your
own marketing magic.

This upcoming section is just for *you*.

It has three segments: Applying the
Culture, Applying the Compensation,
and Applying the Process.

Good luck.

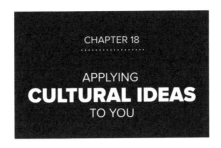

A ssessing the culture of your company is difficult. It isn't as simple as asking the employees if they like the place they work or feel comfortable there. Here are some tools that may help you begin.

Answer these Yes or No questions to evaluate your company's culture.

1. Do you trust your people?
2. Do your people trust you?
3. Do your people trust each other?

Seriously, if you don't get anything else from this section, ask these questions about trust and get real answers. Getting to three yeses on those will help more than anything else you could do.

But I have more for you anyway. Here are some questions to help you evaluate your company's

A great place to look

for how to ask hard questions is the book *Good Leaders Ask Great Questions* by John Maxwell (honestly, nearly everything by Maxwell is terrific). It can help you figure out not only what questions to ask, but how to go about asking them. Another highly recommended title is *Find Out Anything From Anyone, Anytime* by Maryann Karinch and James Pyle. It's a little more on the interrogation side, but that could come in handy.

culture. The more Yes answers you have, the more harmony, creativity, and autonomy are encouraged at your company.

1. Do your people feel comfortable brainstorming with each other? Even with people "above" them?
2. When an obstacle arises, is the team response to figure out a solution? Are questions used to understand the situation rather than to infer blame?
3. Is your building built for cooperation? Are there spaces that not only allow but encourage team discussion and collaboration? Are there physical and digital spaces where team members can simultaneously contribute to and deliberate on projects in real time? Harmon Brothers uses Slack to communicate and collaborate digitally. It works very well.
4. Do your people feel like they have the freedom to express their individual personalities and interests in the workplace, such as furnishing their work area?
5. Can you trust your people to be honest (with both time and money), and can you trust their judgement enough to throw out typical company rules over dress and professional behavior? In other words, can you trust your people to adult?
6. Do your people have flexibility with their work schedule? Is telecommuting allowed?
7. Are the meetings you hold valuable and useful to all who attend? Are those meetings short and focused?
8. Does your culture easily accommodate individual needs of your people (e.g., health- or family-related issues)?
9. Do the people who leave your company leave on good terms?

10. Does your culture encourage people to want to stay? Do people feel validated, valued, and feel like they are progressing both personally and within their career?
11. Do you have a waiting list of people wanting to work for your company? Do they want to work there badly enough that they'll take less than standard wages or even offer to work for free to prove themselves?

It takes guts and courage to ask these hard questions. That's why I wished you luck.

The more Yes answers you have to the questions above, the better. But don't let these be the only questions you ask—use these as a starting point, like Danny Ocean scoping out the Bellagio—once you have the blueprints and a plan, you still have to go in there and steal the $160 million. And the girl.

Okay, not my best analogy. You know what I mean.

Your goal is to discern where your culture encourages your best people to stay, contribute, and grow within your company, and where your culture cages your best people (because, inevitably, Jurassic Park staff will one day turn off the containment fields and the dinosaurs will eat you).

Survey your staff.

Technology makes it quite easy to take the temperature of your workplace.

If hierarchy is part of your company culture, then an anonymous online survey can be most valuable (there are dozens of good options for building these electronic surveys). Try scale questions. These can tell you more than binary, yes/no questions.

Here is a survey to start from—tailor it to what you need. Mechanically, you can set this up in a Google Form where all responses are anonymous. That will definitely encourage greater honest feedback.

May the odds be in your favor.

A Sample Survey to Gauge Company Culture

On a scale from 1 to 10, 1 being "No, not a chance" and 10 being "Yes, seriously, always," please respond to this anonymous survey in order to help us make this company a better place to work. If any answers need explanation, please feel free to write on this page. Your voice matters to us, and we value your input and your contribution to our company.

1. I speak my opinions, even if they're contrary to the direction of the company.

   No 1   2   3   4   5   6   7   8   9   10 Yes

2. I voice objections or disagree with my coworkers on projects without someone getting offended.

   No 1   2   3   4   5   6   7   8   9   10 Yes

3. I can prove I'm accomplishing my work without a time card.

   No 1   2   3   4   5   6   7   8   9   10 Yes

4. Our company's meetings are valuable to my particular job.

   No 1   2   3   4   5   6   7   8   9   10 Yes

5. I will definitely be staying at this company for another year.

   No 1 2 3 4 5 6 7 8 9 10 Yes

6. Our office space makes collaboration and asking questions easy to do.

   No 1 2 3 4 5 6 7 8 9 10 Yes

7. When a problem arises on a project, people focus on solutions rather than blame.

   No 1 2 3 4 5 6 7 8 9 10 Yes

8. I feel like my work is valued.

   No 1 2 3 4 5 6 7 8 9 10 Yes

9. I feel like I am progressing in the company, both personally and within my career.

   No 1 2 3 4 5 6 7 8 9 10 Yes

10. This company accommodates my personal situations without risking my job.

    No 1 2 3 4 5 6 7 8 9 10 Yes

11. My coworkers are honest with both money and time on the job.

    No 1 2 3 4 5 6 7 8 9 10 Yes

12. What is not working here at the company? (This is your chance to help us fix anything that needs fixing.)

    No 1 2 3 4 5 6 7 8 9 10 Yes

13. What is working here at this company? (We need to know what to keep—we don't want to ruin anything that's going great here.)

No 1   2   3   4   5   6   7   8   9   10   Yes

14. What is your favorite number between No and Yes?

No 1   2   3   4   5   6   7   8   9   10   Yes

Of course, the higher the scores on this survey, the more flexible and attractive your company culture is to smart creatives, and the more likely they'll stay.

Changing the culture of a company has far-reaching consequences for productivity, turnover, and job satisfaction. It will free you to unlock more creativity and innovation. And who knows, your employees might start liking work again.

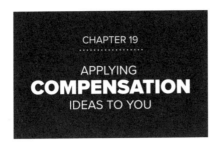

A re you wondering if this compensation format might work for your company?
Answer the questions below. If you can answer Yes to the majority of them, your company has the potential for a redesign that could unleash more creativity and a better culture than your company has ever experienced.

Revenue

- Can your company measure the revenue each project brings into the overall stream?
- Can the costs of each project be measured accurately, over and above the standard business overhead (those costs you incur irrespective of the particular project)?
- Can the ongoing impact of each project be measured over time?

Compensation

- Is the compensation of the company's employees flexible, that is, *not* tied to a rigid scale (i.e., predetermined tiers of pay for certain organizational levels, educational backgrounds, or longevity)?
- Does your compensation plan have the flexibility to reward employees with bonuses or other increased compensation?

- Are rewards and compensation tied to performance of specific tasks as opposed to nonproductive individual characteristics, such as degrees or certifications?

Communication

- Do members of the project team have the ability to communicate freely so that each member can see the work of others?
- Do the members of the team have a sufficient level of understanding of the tasks of other groups (e.g., marketing-to-programming, quality control-to-manufacturing, etc.) so that they can understand the impact of other skill sets on the overall success of the project?
- Is there a forum where each component of the project can show its contributions for general view (or are the project's components hidden from one another)?
- Do your employees have a pressure-free space to voice concerns, or have they learned Klingon so they can complain to each other about managers without fear of reprimand?

"vIHtaHbogh pIn bep?"

If you can answer Yes or Hisl'aH to most of the above questions, your company is a strong candidate for this innovative compensation model. If your answers aren't mostly Yes, don't despair. This is just the beginning. There are more innovative ideas to come— check out Harmon Brothers University and their other educational content.

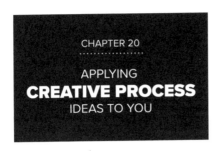

Creative Process almost sounds counterintuitive— shouldn't creative work just happen?

But we have seen that it doesn't.

Remember the four important ingredients to a Creative Process: Flexibility, Measurability, Control, and Trust. Answering the following questions should help you narrow down where your system fosters and encourages creativity, and where you might have blocks.

Do you have a consistent process for creative development?

In the production of a video, Harmon Brothers has a tightly controlled process to handle workflow. Mozart had a specific place he did his work—sitting at his piano. Magician Penn Jillette reads and writes in the bathtub for hours at time. Sir Winston Churchill did the same, which is the beginnings of a pattern. What's *your* creative bathtub?

- Does your company, whatever its product, have a defined creative process?
- Do you have a place that encourages creative flow?
- Do you budget the necessary time to generate ideas?
- Do you know the steps needed to mold your rough ideas into something polished and useful?

- Do you have a deadline to motivate you to action as well as to conclude your creativity?

Do you have space for creativity in non-creative projects?

Google famously allowed its engineers to spend time thinking broadly about the products it offered, and one result was Gmail. In one sense, this is an odd product for a company known for its search engine, but it has dramatically expanded the reach of the company. Additionally, Google has managed a fresh take on a decidedly unsexy product—email.

- Similarly, if your product is something defined, say, making a bathroom stool, for which there is a strict checklist, are there ways to encourage creative thinking?
- Are there ways you can reimagine a core product?
- Are there other products your company could produce?
- Are there complimentary products that attach to the main one, which your company could sell along with it (known in business circles as vertical markets)?
- Is there a culture of creativity at your company?

Is there room to deviate from the creative process if that becomes wise?

The normal process for a Harmon Brothers ad is to try out a company's products, the team becomes a fan, and then agrees to create an ad for that company.

> **The book** Harmon Brothers would recommend here is Russell Brunson's *DotCom Secrets* or possibly *Expert Secrets*. Partly because ClickFunnels (Russell's company) is a Harmon Brothers client, but mainly because the book is a terrific explanation of web-based upselling and marketing.

In the ClickFunnels project, that process was turned around. Harmon Brothers agreed to create a script in exchange for ClickFunnels' help solving a website conversion problem, and then ended up loving the script and product after the fact, so they decided to create a hero ad for ClickFunnels.

Harmon Brothers tries to follow their own good advice, to change the order of their Creative Process if it seems wise.

Nearly everyone that does regular creative work has a process through which they like to accomplish that work. Hopefully these questions help you determine your company's Creative Process strengths and weaknesses.

WHEN THE
DUST SETTLES

{ *Can the principles of how to do things*
hold up under the stress of doing them? }

One of my least favorite story endings of all time is the fable of "The Grasshopper and the Ant."

In case you skipped Aesop's famous fables in elementary school, the story goes like this: a diligent colony of ants works all summer to store food for winter. Alongside them is a grasshopper, and all he does is play the violin. He does no "work."

By and by, the winter comes. The grasshopper looks about and can find no food. It has all been buried by the snow. Famished, he knocks on the door of the colony and begs them to feed him. The ants are boring, but well-fed, having been both diligent and wise. The ants tell the grasshopper that if he's hungry, he should keep his belly full by playing his violin. He starves to death.

And then the ant teenagers riot because they have no music to listen to, and they burn the grain, and all the ants starve to death too (this last part does not actually happen, but, being a grasshopper myself, it always felt to me like it should).

There's a moral to the story, but I don't have to tell you what it is, do I? American culture is strongly, overwhelmingly, ant.

Powerful work ethics are lauded. Scenes of "The Tortoise and the Hare" (another of Aesop's fables) are replayed for us endlessly.

And look, there's good reason for this. Persistent hard work is a powerful thing. Diligent focus is a critical factor in success. But it's not all there is to life. As A.A. Milne (of Winnie the Pooh fame) once wrote, in his essay "The Case for the Artist,"

"The bee devotes its whole life to preparing for the next generation . . . What do the bees think that they are doing? If they live a life of toil and self-sacrifice merely in order that the next generation may live a life of equal toil and self-sacrifice?"

If the entire and only point of our working like bees is so that we can make more bees who do the same . . . then is all of this actually worth it? This is a case against an ant-only lifestyle.

At the same time, we have the celebration of the idea that the only thing that matters is the show, and the show comes from nowhere, striking like lightning from a clear sky. You don't have to work at it. You *can't* work at it. The muse either comes or she doesn't. A creative must be unfettered by rules and systems, free to create whatever comes to mind and heart—ideally supported by tax dollars, so that the genius need not sully himself with crass commercialism. This is a case against a grasshopper-only lifestyle.

But what if there were a different fable, and a different moral to the story—one that recognizes the power of art and the potency of work, and the multiplied strength of both together?

If the grasshopper is going to be good at his music, he's going to have to work very hard at it. And if the ants never take time

FROM POOP TO GOLD

to let down their antennae, they won't need their teenagers to riot—they'll keel over from sheer exhaustion.

But let's say the ants and the grasshoppers had a confab. Let's say they came up with a set of principles that would allow as much work as possible to be done while playing, and as much play as possible to mix with the work.

Let's say those principles are:

Creative Culture

Everyone works hard: The grasshoppers at their creativity, the ants with their deadlines. They review each other's work and make suggestions. They listen to each other. Everyone's ideas get a hearing. The sharing out of the food values every contribution to the harvest. And the sharing is sorted by the workers, not just the queen.

Creative Process

The grasshoppers' creativity is encouraged and celebrated. The ants set deadlines and haul food. Both are valued and seen as necessary to get the harvest in before the snow flies.

Creative Partnerships

The ants and the grasshoppers set up a farm stand selling their world-class food and encouraging customers to buy with enticing marketing—I mean music. Sales shoot through the roof until the booth sells out and customers tell their neighbors about the anthopper experience.

And the bugs inherit the earth. The end.

Harmon Brothers, who are often lauded in particular for their comedic creativity, uses these three principles every day.

The marketing magic at Harmon Brothers had to be crafted. It took work. It also took play. The one without the other would have produced nothing of value. But both together? In a sort of alchemy, the poop turns into gold.

FROM POOP TO GOLD

Acknowledgements

On this project (as in all of my work) the ground is littered with the bodies of those who tried to drag my sorry carcass across the finish line. I get my name on the cover, and they get mentioned here at the end, which is spectacularly unfair, because without them there wouldn't be a book at all.

Thank you to the entire Harmon Brothers team who let me peek into their offices, procedures, principles, and lives, often without my having asked permission—especially when lunch was served. For the record, I did not switch Luke's head onto Chewie's body that one day, but I know who did. Sorry, Daniel and Shane, I'm no snitch.

Long before the end was in sight, I had two people metaphorically pump blood into me: Elizabeth Schulte and Tim Ziegler. Lyz is a gifted editor and writer in her own right, and her touch is everywhere in this book. You won't see it, because she's so gentle and organic to the process, but it's there. Tim, blessings on his soul, took what was a middling piece of text and said, "This could be seriously great. Think bigger." Without him, you wouldn't be reading this.

Then at the point where we had to limp back to Dodge City or go on to El Dorado, Mandy S. grabbed the reins and drove the stagecoach. She deserves credit as wide as the New Mexico sky.

Down the stretch, I had the indispensable help of a whole team of skilled wordsmiths: Valerie H., lead editor and *the* most terrifyingly astute editor I've ever suffered being corrected by; Tiffani B., whose skills are so multifaceted and various it would be impossible to list them all; and Kellen Erskine, who is very funny in person, on stage, and in print. Any jokes in here that don't work for you are my fault. He tried to fix them.

Special thanks to my beta readers: Nick R., Jake C., Brad S., Josh L., Chad M., Luke M., Tyler E., Tyler B., Kevin W., and Teiko R., and Marci C. performed a brilliant edit as the clock ticked to zero. You're a genius, lady, and I'm grateful.

The design of the book was a significant challenge, and I must thank Daniel H. for the cover, Brett C. for the timeline design and fonts, Daniel R. for the typesetting, and Alex B. for the caricatures. For the record, mine looks just like me. Dead on.

It would probably be wise to conclude with thanks to my longsuffering family, especially my sweet love Jeanette, who will

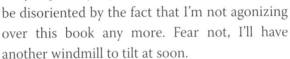

be disoriented by the fact that I'm not agonizing over this book any more. Fear not, I'll have another windmill to tilt at soon.

Until then, my friends—

CJ

Appendix:

The Harmon Brothers Organizational Chart

Benton Crane	**Daniel Harmon**
Chief Executive Officer *(CEO)* *& Founder*	*Chief Creative Officer* *(CCO)* *& Founder*

Admin Team	**Funnel Team**
Katie Camilletti *Office Manager*	Brett Crockett *Funnel Team Lead*
Dave Sullivan *Finance Director*	Mandy Shepherd *Brand Strategy Manager*
Gavin Bentley *Head of Operations*	Cory Stevens *Ad Buyer & Data Analyst*
Matthew Faraci *Public Relations*	Jordan Allen *CRO Specialist & Web Developer*
	Jake Christensen *Optimization Editor* *& Motion Graphics*
	Morgan Reber *Social Media Manager*

FROM POOP TO GOLD

Growth Team

Kurt Horn
Growth Team Lead

Theron Harmon
Growth Team Lead

Former HB Team Members

Brett Stubbs
Tech Lead

Jonah Rindlisbacher
Producer/Editor

Abe Niederhauser
Lead Media Buyer

Brooke Newbold
Ad Buyer

Creative Team

Shane Rickard
Creative Director

James Dayton
Creative Director

Jonny Vance
Creative Director & Writer

Tiffani Barth
Project Manager

Josh Stofferahn
Lead Producer

Dave Vance
Lead Writer

Kaitlin Snow Seamons
Lead Video Editor

Tyler Stevens
Director of Photography & VFX

Mike Henderson
Postproduction Omnivore & BTS

Nick Ritter
Lead VFX

Bryson Alley
Postproduction Carnivore

Founders & Advisors

Jeffrey Harmon

Neal Harmon

INTRODUCING:

HARMON BROTHERS
UNIVERSITY

Dear Reader,

Daniel Harmon here. Thank you for reading our book!

(You didn't steal it from someone, right?)

I hope that this is the best book you've ever read that contains the word "Poop" in the title.

But more importantly, I hope that you learned something that you can apply to your personal life and/or your business.

I want to personally invite you to join myself and our lead writer, Dave Vance, as we pull back the curtain to reveal how Harmon Brothers consistently creates videos that delight, entertain—and most importantly, videos that sell.

A hint? It starts with the script.

The Harmon Brothers University foundational course, *Write Ads That Sell*, will give you the exact same step-by-step, principle-by-principle breakdown, methods, formulas and training that all of our writers receive before they work on an HB campaign.

As we developed this course, our motto was literally, "hold nothing back." In Write Ads that Sell, each of the 25+ lessons were designed with your success in mind. This course is the culmination of millions of dollars invested in research and development through the trial and error of making ads that have sold hundreds of millions of dollars for our clients.

Join us as we reveal:

SECRET #1:	SECRET #2:	SECRET #3:
Videos don't have to be viral to sell.	*Humor is great, but it's not the goal.*	*You can do this on your budget.*
In fact, we explain why trying for viral is exactly the WRONG approach if you want your video to sell—and what to do instead to maximize the reach of your content.	Our videos usually use humor to sell—but even more important than the jokes are the formulas we use. We're sharing the exact structure we use to generate millions of dollars in sales for our clients.	You don't have to have a large production budget to do what we do. Sure, it helps—but you'll learn the keys that will enable you to create a successful campaign on any budget.

Apply today at:

⬈ HarmonBrothersUniversity.com